Pain – My Friend

by

Edward M. Guziejka

Edward M. Guziejka

Copyright © 2004 by Edward M. Guziejka

ISBN 0-7414-0718-3

Published by:

INFIᗯITY
PUBLISHING.COM

Infinity Publishing.com
519 West Lancaster Avenue
Haverford, PA 19041-1413
Info@buybooksontheweb.com
www.buybooksontheweb.com
Toll-free (877) BUY BOOK
Local Phone (610) 520-2500
Fax (610) 519-0261

Printed in the United States of America

Printed on Recycled Paper

Published March, 2004

Dedicated

to

Charley

ACKNOWLEDGMENTS

Joy Pringle, England; Father Lucius, U.S.A.; Paul Truesdell, Okinawa, Japan; Evelyn Kalchas, Izmir, Turkey; Frank Reifsnyder, England; Robbie Morgan, Iceland; Steve Givens, U.S.A.; Ava DeLorenzo, U.S.A.; and Janet Moran Neil, England, whose dedication to "would be" writers cannot be fully appreciated, unless you sit in on her classes!

My children, Susan, Eric, and Amy, for their constant love and understanding.

My wife, Mary ... what can I say? Without her, there would be no *Pain – My Friend.*

BIOGRAPHY

Edward Guziejka is a first generation American whose family emigrated from Poland. He and his five brothers were World War II veterans. Later, Mary and Edward married and raised three children, Susan, Eric and Amy. In the midst of raising children and studying to be a Plastics Engineer, all his dreams crashed. Four spinal operations, pain, depression, alcohol and drugs dictated his days over the next many years. Despair filled his life until the Pain Unit changed the pattern. 'Pain-My Friend' is a result of unsuccessful operations, medical failures, and Edward's urgent need to help others.

To And Fro

I have been north, as far north as north will go,
Where there is no east or west.
I have been south, as far south as south will go,
Where there is no west or east.
I go to and fro, to and fro.

When I was north, as far north as north will go,
I took one step south,
There I saw east meeting west.
I go round and around I go.

When I was south, as far south as south will go,
I took one step north,
There I saw west meeting east.
I go round and around I go.

I have been south, as far south as south will go,
Where there is no west or east.
I have been north, as far north as north will go,
Where there is no east or west.
I go to and fro, to and fro.

Edward M. Guziejka

TABLE OF CONTENTS

> *Always dost thou wax and wane Detestable life.*
> **Thou dost withdrew my health and virtue,**
> **thou dost threaten my emotion and weakness with torture.**
> *At this hour, therefore, let us pluck the strings without delay.*
> *Let us mourn together, for fate crushes the brave.*
> "Carmina Burana"
> Karl Orff

1

TOO OLD

I knew the moment I dragged my left leg into my neurosurgeon's office that he didn't want to see me. When I limped in, he turned in his chair to face the window behind him. Then he turned back to face me.

"You're too old!" he said sternly. "You're too old for physical therapy! Go home! Stop wasting your time and money! Start getting used to the idea that you're going to spend most of your time in bed. There's nothing else we can do. Any more operations on your back will only increase your inability to do as little as you are doing now. Go home. Do as I say."

I didn't know the color of my pain, but there in that doctor's drab office, red was as vivid as it could be. I was angry! In active pain, only forty, and with a family to support, I sat, as this man who called himself a doctor told me to go home. I was too old. He couldn't do anything for me.

Yet, on my first visit, he was so sure of himself. He proudly pointed to pictures, hanging on his office walls, of his successes with royal patients and movie stars. He exhibited no failures.

Mary was in the waiting room. I had to tell her something, but what? How could I tell her that our lives were virtually over? How could I tell her that I would never work again and would be in bed for the rest of my life? How could I tell her to continue being the mother, the father, the shopper, the doer, and now the only breadwinner? How could I tell her that all our dreams from the years before we got married would never be realized?

What should I tell my children? Climb up on my bed my little boy? My son, run and fetch for me? Do for me my little girls? Reverse the roles for the next twenty or thirty years, or until I die.

Mary came into the examining room, not smiling, but deep in anxiety, with apprehension written all over her face.

"Well? What did he say?" she asked.

As usual, I didn't know what to say. She repeated her question in an exasperated manner, louder this time and with a sour expression on her face. "Well ... tell me! What did he say? Is he going to give you physical therapy? Is he going to prescribe something to help you get going? He must be going to do SOMETHING!" She pounded it out like a jackhammer.

I looked at her, then muttered, "He said to go home. He said to stay in bed and get used to it. Nothing can be done for me. I'm too old."

"NOTHING? Nothing can be done? Go to bed and stay there? He actually said that?" Like me, Mary couldn't believe the doctor's diagnosis. She turned on her heel, picked up my discarded clothes, pacing back and forth, and yelled at me. "What did you say to him? Didn't you say anything at all? Did you let him tell you that? Anyone knows that no one is too old for some kind of physical therapy."

Again, the jackhammer voice was rat-a-tat-tatting away at me. I shut it out. I didn't bother to listen anymore. We'd been through it all before, with many different doctors. The only difference was that this one said I was too old. That was a new wrinkle for my sagging, almost destroyed mind.

Mary kept it up. "Who's going to take care of you? I can't—anymore! How much more can I? As it is, I do everything. How much more can be expected?" She slumped into a chair with her arms and my clothes folded tightly around her.

"I'm sorry, Ed. I really am sorry," she muttered finally.

Sympathy and understanding were the two commodities we were running out of in our home, along with money. Slowly donning my clothes, I limped out of that dreary brown room, leaving it bleak and red with anger. The room belonged to a stupid doctor, who had the audacity to tell me nothing more could be done for my pain. I would have to live with it? God! Why me? I screamed silently. We left the tall building and became lost in the shadows, afraid to wonder what the future had in store for us. When we reached the parking lot, Mary bolted ahead. She dashed to the driver's side of our compact car, opened the door, sat in the driver's seat, and said, "I'll drive." I tried to explain how driving could distract me from the pain, but she wasn't convinced. She kept insisting that she would drive.

"I'm sorry, Ed." She warned, "You have already taken two percodans for your pain."

"So what?" I snapped.

Mary explained, "Your pain medication might dull your reflexes; it's no different than drinking and driving. Couple it with the anxiety caused by what the doctor told you and you will understand why I must drive. Besides, I can see how much pain you're in. You're in no condition to get behind the wheel."

There was no other choice but to brace my body for thirty miles of random jolts on our return home. Our car was a compact, not designed for comfort. The least road imperfection vibrated pain through my back. My thoughts went to Jim from whom we had bought the car.

"You know Mary," I said, "I wish now we had listened to Jim and hadn't bought this compact car."

"Yes, he said you wouldn't like it. It was too small and you wouldn't be comfortable in it, remember?"

I remembered, "I know, I know. That's what happens when you try to save money."

Words seemed to elude us for the rest of the trip. My only thoughts were of home and of my increasingly urgent need to lie down on my bed. The lack of conversation, the silence, and the car's jolting ride made the trip seem longer than usual. Finally Mary pulled into our driveway and came to a stop.

She rushed out as usual. I sat there alone, desolate, in grief and despair, trying to figure how to get out of the car without making my pain worse. I struggled with my body, gave up, and continued to sit, pondering my fate.

I have a pain that never leaves me, stays with me day and night, a pain that becomes worse with each operation, a pain that gathers speed and grows in intensity to a full force with a burning, agitating, mind-damaging roar, and only abates, never disappears, until I lie down. My life consists of pills and alcohol, alcohol and pills—and my bed. Nothing matters anymore. I am now too old for physical therapy. My only hope. Now, I have nothing left.

Somehow, I got out of the car. When I got into the house, the first thing I did was to take three percodans with a shot of whiskey. Then I got a glass of orange juice from the fridge. One at a time I climbed the stairs to my bedroom, favoring my left leg, hanging on to the banister, the pain burning and searing. Even with my mind preoccupied with manipulating the stairs, the doctor's words echoed, "You're too old for physical therapy. You're too old for physical therapy." A gnawing began inside of me. It formed a knot in my stomach. Then tightness started to torment the back of my neck, adding to my already intolerable back pain.

Once in my bedroom, I automatically turned on the stereo. It was the first thing I always did. Carl Orff's "Carmina Burana," a favorite of mine, continued from the point where it had been turned off earlier.

How strange it was that the music and the words coincided with my feelings! I joined in with the chorus, as I often did while the music resounded with the agony and pain I was experiencing. Then I waited. I stood in front of the stereo, with both arms draped over the dresser, and my head slumped on my arms, waiting for the drums and the chorus. Finally, they came. The drums and cymbals crashed my feelings into the loud brasses and chorus. Lifting my head, I sang. I sang louder. I screamed, *"O Fortuna velut luna statu variabilis."*

The music softened to, *"Semper crescis aut decrescis; vita detestabilis."* The softened beat abruptly detracted from the intensity of my feelings. I wasn't finished! It wasn't enough! Automatically, I caught the beat once again and let it work up to its final crescendo.

At times, I sang ahead impatiently, then stopped and waited for the beat to catch up. The waiting was exasperating. My need for an immediate release was too strong for it.

My pain took hold. I stiffened; the burning and full force of the pain grabbed me. It came. It came, and I let go, pounding on the dresser and screaming with the chorus, *"Sors salutis et virtutis michi nunc contraria, est effectus et defectus semper in angaria. Hac in hora sine mora corde pulsum tangite; quod per sortem sternit fortem, mecum omnes plangite!"* I let the drums and voices melt into my feelings until tears flowed.

Exhausted, I dropped onto my bed and stared at the ceiling. My cat leaped up and made herself comfortable on my stomach, expecting her strokes. I looked into her green eyes, "Why me? Why in hell me?" She didn't answer. I closed my eyes and went into a deep sleep.

2

INTRACTABLE PAIN

As the days passed, Mary and I continued our usual routine of arguing about what I did, or didn't do, or how much I drank and how we never had enough money to do anything else. Mary's bitterness and resentment showed up more and more in our day-to-day affairs.

Monday arrived. That night was our weekly group session night. We had become involved in these sessions when we took our daughter to the Mental Health Clinic because of her misbehaviors. In time we discovered that Mary and I were the ones who needed the help. We had been attending these meetings for months, hoping to restore some sanity to our daily existence.

In Mary's opinion, group therapy sessions smacked of shame and failure. It was difficult for her to talk freely and intimately in front of a group of strangers.

I didn't mind the sessions and often wondered why. It was comforting for me to share my back pain experiences with others. I had no trouble talking freely and intimately with the members of our group, or with anyone else. Group sessions and hospitals had become my world, my stage, my play.

When Mary and I arrived at the Mental Health Clinic, we went through our usual greetings with the three other couples. Then, everyone took a seat in the circle of chairs set up for us.

Dr. Ellis entered. Again, with the usual greetings, he took his seat in the circle. Mary had phoned Dr. Ellis earlier to bring him up to date on what happened at the neurosurgeon's office.

Dr. Ellis asked, "Mary, will you tell ..."

Immediately, Mary broke in, "Can you imagine a doctor telling your husband he's too old for physical therapy? He's only forty years old. And then saying, there is nothing else he can do? My husband has to get used to the idea that he must remain in bed for most of the rest of his life? Can you imagine any doctor saying that? What are we supposed to do? He said there's nothing else that can be done." Her voice broke and she began to cry.

For a minute the room was dead silent. Then someone said, "Ed, aren't you going to console her?"

"Console her for what? She always cries," I replied.

A woman got up, took out a Kleenex from her bag and brought it to Mary, "Go ahead and cry Mary. It will make you feel good."

I watched. Then I said, "She's always crying. I get sick and tired of it. I'm the one who's sick and I'm not crying! And I don't intend to stay in bed for the rest of my life! I'm certainly not there now, am I? I shifted my body around trying to find comfortable position in my chair, pain tearing through my body and hollered, "I don't understand! I just don't understand ...Why me?"

I needed a cigarette and was about to light up. Dr. Ellis reminded me that there was no smoking. I didn't think I could stay there much longer without one.

Mary continued crying.

Dr. Ellis, a shy, unassertive, polite man, twisted and turned in his chair, cleared his throat nervously and said, "Ed, Dr. Holt, a friend of mine, opened a Pain Unit at a Rehabilitation Hospital not too far from here. I would be happy to call him for you, if you think you would be interested."

In anguish I tried to talk through my pain and said, "I read something about a Pain Unit, somewhere. What's a Pain Unit?" I caught my breath and held it for a while.

He answered, "It's exactly what the name implies, Ed. The Unit accepts only those people who are in constant pain, and unable to do useful work, or lead a normal daily life. Their pain is intractable. Intractable ..."

I interrupted, "What was that again, intracta ... what?"

"Intractable Pain, it's the same condition you ..."
Again, not letting him finish, I asked, "Intractable pain, that's what I've got? What does intractable mean?"

"It means that nothing can relieve the pain. It's chronic pain that has no remedy or cure, unlike acute pain which has a remedy or cure." Dr. Ellis pushed his glasses back up on his nose and continued, "That is the reason why the doctor told you to start getting used to the idea of staying in bed to relieve the pain."

"What do they do at a Pain Unit?" I asked. I could see that the other members were just as interested in finding out as I was.

Dr. Ellis continued, "Dr. Holt, who runs the Pain Unit, was a neurosurgeon. He knew his surgeries for back pain were not successful. Ninety-nine percent of the patients who had his spinal surgeries came back feeling worse. He felt his surgical techniques were a failure and decided to become a psychiatrist."

At that point, all of us in the circle of chairs were giving our complete attention to every word this nervous but caring man uttered.

Dr. Ellis spoke slowly and deliberately. "He found that he could teach his patients how to deal with their pain by using behavior modification. He feels that our reaction to pain is a learned process. Therefore, if it is learned, then it can be unlearned. In Asia and Africa, some tribes react differently than we do to pain. They can walk on hot coals without getting burned. They can insert items into their lips and noses, and a host of other body parts without reacting to pain as we do. Pain does not cripple them."

And then Dr. Ellis delivered a blow. He said, "Dr. Holt's patients are interviewed to determine whether they are willing to go through the rigors of the Unit's treatments. My only fear is that you may not be accepted."

Mary looked aghast. She was incredulous! The words flew out of her mouth, "Is it really possible Ed might not be accepted because his body isn't in enough pain?"

I listened intently, as did the others, but I really didn't know what Dr. Holt meant. This behavior thing meant nothing to me. To change my reaction to pain was equally meaningless. I did sense a certain excitement about going to another hospital. Was it a sense of relief to my dilemma? I didn't think so. It was something stranger than that. Maybe it was the attention I would get.

Mary and I tried to pull ourselves together to leave. Getting up and leaving was always a chore. We both agreed that Dr. Ellis should pursue this course and call us as soon as possible. We bid goodnight to all and drove away through the darkness.

On the way home I said, "Something must be wrong with the battery. Suddenly our headlights seem to be brighter."

Mary quickly disagreed. "No they're not. What do you mean?"

I just shrugged. I couldn't quite explain it. A glimmer of hope was beginning to shine within me, but I didn't quite trust it. I wouldn't allow it to get out of control, just in case the Pain Unit turned out to be another disappointment. That would be terrible. "It won't happen again," I said to myself as I drove home.

When we arrived at our house, Mary got out of the car, leaving me to drive her mother, our babysitter, home. If nothing else, I could at least drive my car. Upon my return, Mary had readied herself for bed and taken care of the children.

She always read to the children every night, sang with them and kissed them at bedtime, no matter when it was.

Bedtime was a very special time in our family. Age of child, or time of night was of no importance. Susan was sixteen at this time, in a room of her own, and Eric was eleven. He shared a room with his baby sister, Amy, who was then only two years old. We were a close, loving family. Mary was very affectionate. Family was the most important thing in her life. The guilt Mary had at leaving her children daily to teach music in a nearby town nagged at her constantly. Spending most evenings with me in the hospital made Mary's guilt almost unbearable. Her mother and father, who cared for the children, were the only ones who could make Mary comfortable.

Unconsciously, she was also my surrogate for kissing the children goodnight. My pain wouldn't allow me to bend over for kisses.

Emotionally and physically the group sessions were difficult for me. It was easy for me to discuss my feelings on pain. My four back operations plus seven surgeries in other areas gave me enough material to talk about. But, my insecurity on various other subjects always prevailed. I did not like to be noticed. I was a shy person. Will I misuse my words? Will they laugh at what I say? Will my poor high-school grades be noticed? A high-school education was all I had managed. Mary, a teacher with a degree in music, was the educated one. I always relied on her to know all the answers.

My pain forced me to change positions often. I went from sitting to standing, or walked around the circle of participants. The mental and physical stresses exhausted all my energy to fight the pain. For me, the two-hour meeting was like digging ditches for eight hours. It was impossible to keep the pain away and deal with the reversed roles that were part of our family. Dad was at home, and Mother was teaching at school. Mary left for work every morning.

I developed a habit of surrounding myself with music. The classics and many popular musical scores were always playing, no matter where or when. This time, the more the pain hurt, the more thought went into deciding what tape was to be played—a Beethoven, a Chopin, a Mozart, a musical or some popular music. I decided on playing a Beethoven. I loved the second movement of the "Concerto Number 5."

Along with two percodans and a double shot of Canadian whiskey, the music would be a soothing ritual. All my bedtime preparations could be accomplished during the first movement of the concerto. Thcn, I would be free to listen uninterruptedly to the remainder of my choice. I knew that the second movement's slow deliberate notes, ingeniously written to create a dialogue between piano and orchestra, would create a state of relaxation. The volume was turned down, so as not to disturb our children.

While changing into my pajamas, a thought flashed across my mind. Pain Unit! I remembered a newspaper clipping cut out months ago. My memory was distorted and fuzzy, the percodan and liquor overtaking the pain, but it finally focused on where the clipping was. "The top drawer," I said. My important clippings were always placed in the top drawer.

The clipping seemed to jump out from underneath a box sitting on top. Nothing in that drawer was ever found easily, but there it was, showing a picture of a smiling man from a Pain Unit. He was holding a device used to prevent pain. The headlines read, "TRANSCUTANEOUS DEVICE HELPS PATIENT GO BACK TO WORK."

I read what was written, then decided to share it with Mary. I shook the clipping at her, to draw her attention to it. At that moment, my favorite part of the concerto began. I lay on the bed with my right arm bent, still holding onto the clipping. I allowed each slow deliberate note to create goose-bumps down my spine and up through the back of my head. What my body was feeling from the effects of that music was better than pain-killing pills. It was euphoria and I was in it. It was sadness, beauty. What a masterpiece! The timing was perfect.

Mary's attention was drawn to the clipping I still held. I let it fall to her side of the bed.

"What is it?" she asked.

I couldn't answer.

"Ed, what are you doing?

Still, no answer from me.

"ED!" she shouted. "What do you want?"

"Sorry!" I said. "You know, in one week's time strange signs have occurred. I was told I was too old and I translated "Carmina Burana" and found out about '*O fortuna*'. Coming home from the Mental Health Clinic, our car's headlights seemed to be brighter.

"Tonight, I remembered the article about a Pain Unit. I found it, then my favorite part of the concerto started in. This is all very strange, Mary. It's as if someone up there is telling us that we are doing the right thing. What do you think?"

"I don't know," she said. "I really don't know." Mary didn't read signs as I did. Again she asked, "What do you want?"

I gave her the clipping and said, "There's something strange going on."

She took the clipping and scanned it saying, "This is very interesting. You did say at the group session that you had heard something about a Pain Unit. How long have you had this?"

"A long time, maybe a year."

"Well, maybe it's nothing but a coincidence, Ed."

Again, I began to experience a peculiar excitement at wanting to go to the Pain Unit.

The following Sunday night the phone rang. Mary answered it. Dr. Ellis had done what he had promised. The psychiatrist from the Pain Unit was calling. Mary talked with him for some time. Her voice echoed up into our bedroom, rising and falling, but no words were decipherable.

After hanging up, she ran upstairs into the bedroom crying. She never walked up and down stairs, she ran. She ran everywhere. She also cried about the least little thing. Her crying frustrated me. It seemed to me that she cried every day lately.

"What's the matter now?" I said gruffly. I never knew what to do for her when she cried even when I was still well. Now that I was sick all the time, her tears had become intolerable.

"He accused me of wanting to get rid of you," she sobbed.

"Who did?" I asked.

"That was Dr. Holt who called. He wouldn't understand why I want you to go to the Pain Unit. He kept asking, why do you want to get rid of your husband? Ed, I don't want to get rid of you. You know in your heart that I don't want to get rid of you. Don't you?"

She lay on the bed next to me, and I held her in my arms.

"I only want you to get better," she broke down. "I want things to be the way they were when we got married."

Mary, inconsolable at this point, rolled herself over to her side of the bed, hiding her head in the pillow. It seemed strange to me that a doctor would say something like that to her.

What would make him think that she wanted to get rid of me? I was sick and needed help. I was sure that was the only reason why she wanted me to go to the Pain Unit.

When Mary's tears were spent, she sat up, propped herself against her pillows, looked at me, and sobbed, "I have to call for a sub. I need to make some lesson plans." Her voice trembled and shook. "You have an appointment for an interview tomorrow, and based on that interview, they'll determine whether or not you qualify as a patient." She wiped her eyes and blew her nose. "I can't imagine you not qualifying. Can you?"

The doctor's critical assessment about Mary wanting to get rid of me by putting me into the Pain Unit made her bitter and angry. Mary always wanted me to go to any hospital that would make me better but, at the same time, she never wanted me to leave her. Love and hate, pain and happiness, always went together in our relationship. One was never far from the other.

And the children—I was losing them. I kept drifting away from them. I was rarely with them. Profound sadness enveloped me when I thought about them. All we could do together was talk, when my mind was working well, that is. Most often these days, I was not able to think because of the intensity of the pain.

Again, that strange excitement fluttered and thrilled inside of me. It was getting stronger and stronger each time I thought of the Pain Unit. It bothered me to know that I wanted to go there. I felt guilty about wanting to leave home, but the feeling couldn't be denied. I wanted to go.

3

COLOR OF PAIN

We arrived for the interview and were escorted to a small room, just big enough to hold a desk and three chairs. Two women were in the room. One, sitting in the chair behind the desk, was introduced as a staff member. The other, to my surprise, was a patient. She was standing next to the staff member.

There were two empty chairs in front of the desk. It was obvious what the seating arrangements were to be. Mary and I took our position next to each other in the empty chairs. While sitting there waiting for the interview to begin, an uncomfortable feeling over came me. It was as if the walls were closing in. I felt a strange pressure in the incision area on my back.

I was alone again with all women, and wondered, where are the men? Something in that room was creating tension within me. Yet we hadn't been there more than three or four minutes. Then the tension began driving itself like a red hot poker into my back, exacerbating the pressure into pain.

Concentrating was going to be difficult. While trying to sort all of this out, I noticed the eye contact directed at me from the staff member. She said, "Do you want to get rid of your pain?"

Shocked and dismayed, I looked at her as if she was nuts. Then, avoiding her eye contact, I said, "Yes! I want to get rid of my pain! What do you think?" I looked at Mary for reinforcement.

She was about to speak but was cut off by the staff member. "Then, why are you holding onto it?"

This time her words bit right into my soul. I could feel that red-hot poker being twisted in my back—the twisting, radiating pain through the bottom half of my body. Again, I avoided her eyes and said, "Holding on to it?" I nearly shouted at her. "I'm not holding onto it! I'm trying to get rid of it. Who the heck wants to hold onto pain?"

"You'd be surprised," said the patient. "How long have you been holding onto your pain?"

"How long? Why do you keep asking me such a stupid question? I don't want it." Then I pleaded, "Don't you understand? I'm not holding onto my pain. I don't want pain." At this point the pain and my anxiety were getting the best of me.

I glanced over at Mary, pleading with my eyes for some support from her. She started to say, "Ed, is ..." but she was rudely interrupted with, "Do you know where your pain is coming from, Ed?"

My plea to Mary distracted me from knowing who'd said it, but my anger was apparent from my flushing face and stiffening body. They wouldn't let Mary say anything. I was in pain, and they didn't care! I wanted to scream. Instead, I explained, "My pain is coming from my back." I hauled myself up from my chair, turned my back toward them and pointed to it. "There—right there—in my back! That's where it is! That's where the pain is coming from!"

"What color is it, and what does it feel like?" Asked the staff member.

Bewildered, I looked at her, sat back down again, and asked, "What color is it? I don't know what color it is! I never knew it had color. What I do know is when the pain enters my back, and it's there now, it feels as if I have been stabbed with a red hot sword. Its blade, like a snake, slithers its way down inside my legs, and finally it bites its way to my toes. Is that what you want to hear?"

There was a pause. The room became dead quiet. I felt as if someone should speak—someone other than me. The quiet was too uncomfortable, so I decided to speak. "What are you people trying to do to me? I didn't know that pain had a color. Now, I wonder if your kind of treatment is for me. Your questions are sure weird. Not once did you ask how I got this way. You seem to be blaming me for having pain." I hollered, "Did you know or do you care to know, that I have had four unsuccessful surgeries on my back? Did you? Did you know that? And you won't even let Mary talk. She can explain everything much better than I."

"No, we're not blaming anyone," said the staff person, as she started her long explanation. The patient standing in back of the desk was nodding in agreement. "The Pain Unit is serious business. Before you can get any comfort from this Pain Unit, you're going to experience more pain than what you have now. We need to be sure that you can handle all the therapies involved. We need to be perfectly sure. That is why the 'weird' questions, Ed. We have a wonderful relaxation program and a heated pool that will help. On the other hand, there are exercises that will add to your pain. There is psychotherapy that will pull out from your unconscious things that will be difficult for you to deal with."

At this point my strength was sapped, I slumped further in my chair and felt like a child being scolded for not understanding.

The staff member's voice carried on, "Knowing what your strengths and weaknesses are is very important to our decision to allow you to participate in the program. We have had people who leave after one week, because the program was too difficult for them. If you don't want to take an active part in the program, then you might as well stay home and continue with your suffering. We cannot get rid of your pain."

I asked myself, what does she mean? She can't get rid of my pain? Why am I here? Why am I sitting here?

"You, and only you, can learn the skills we will introduce. You must constantly apply them so that you will be able to get rid of it, or at least be more comfortable. We know that life can be more positive and fruitful for you, once you've finished the program. This is a program in which your progress is entirely up to you. How much pain and how many skills you keep after finishing the program depend on you. You can say to me that you are willing to do anything to get rid of your pain, but I have to know just how sincere you are. Do your words carry the action that goes with them? I need to know."

With a pause, I felt so defeated, I answered, "All I can say is that I will do whatever is necessary to get rid of my pain so that I can go back to work. I had a wonderful job. I was researching in plastics, developing new uses for missiles, boats and radomes. I loved it. I don't know how else to say it and have it be as convincing to you as you would want it. I want to go back to work. That I do know. That's why I am here for this interview. I want to go back to work."

The interviewers looked at one another and nodded. The staff member spoke, "Okay Ed, we're through with the interview. We'll let you know."

I left the interview feeling guilty about my back problems. The interviewers had completely confused me with what they said about learning skills to ease my pain. Worse still, they hadn't given Mary a chance to say a word. Every time she had tried, they shut her off, directing their barrage of questions at me. Mary might just as well have stayed home and gone to work. To top it off, Dr. Holt wasn't there.

Once in the car, we both looked at each other and simultaneously said, "What do you think?" We really had nothing much to say to each other. The unexpected nature of the interview occupied our entire beings. Was this any worse than being told I was too old for physical therapy? As we drove home, we both fell into a somber mood and reluctantly waited for the results of the interview.

4

ADMITANCE TO REHAB

With the help of Dr. Ellis from the Mental Health Clinic, I was accepted to the Pain Unit. Instead of being delighted, I had second thoughts. I wasn't sure I wanted to go. I would never forget that interview, but Dr. Ellis assured me that the Pain Unit was the right thing for me.

Dr. Ellis was tall and slim, well dressed, well spoken and rather shy. I often wondered how he'd gotten into this business; he was so reserved. In spite of his shyness he was solidly sincere. His sincerity was what held Mary and me together at these meetings. He asked, "What do you have to lose?" He was right. I decided to go.

My bag was packed with pajamas, bathrobe, slippers, toiletries, pad, pen, pencil, radio, and two cartons of cigarettes. Again, as usual, whenever I went to the hospital, my fear of running out of cigarettes became a powerful and unreasonable force. I felt compelled to keep two packs on my person at all times. It became my habit to plead with Mary not to forget to bring more cigarettes every time she visited. I had no fear of running out of pain pills because I knew they would be handed out freely in the hospital. If I needed to I could stack them up, save a few for when I needed a bigger pain fix.

I thought my children were getting used to the idea of Daddy going to hospitals. Nevertheless, Amy, held by her mother as I could no longer pick her up, grabbed onto my neck tightly with both hands and would not let go. She left me, crying her heart out, taken away by her grandmother. Eric choked back tears; his eyes were swimming as he left for school after a long embrace. Susan just held on and would not let go for the longest while. She left crying also. Being the oldest, she seemed to suffer the most. My heart broke. I bade a silent farewell to the house, gave it one last look, and hugged my mother-in-law, who had moved in once again. Somehow, I am not sure how, Mary and I got into our compact car. She drove.

We arrived at the hospital. With great effort, I got out of the car and then leaned on it, trying to relieve my pain. While leaning against the car, I reflected for a moment on the problems left behind at home: the children, my in-laws, Mary, the bills, the nagging, the arguments. It was a relief to know that, once again, decisions would not have to be made by me and my back pain would be taken care of.

While Mary got my things out of the trunk, a strong urge to look to the right of the building overtook me. My eyes seemed to be directed to the high-tension wires at the right corner of a plain, rectangular, red brick building. Then my eyes followed the wires leading up a hill, intermingling with an idled T-Bar used for skiing. It created a maze of shadows against the slope. The many shapes and forms the lines made had an eerie effect on me. Something was telling me that I would climb that hill. I didn't believe it. With my painful body that feat could never be accomplished. I put the thought aside quickly, into the mental file titled: "How to build yourself up for a failure."

We went to the information desk, and they called the Pain Unit. The receptionist said someone would meet us at the Admitting Office next door. We were to go there now.

As I limped to the next door, I glanced around the area. It was very busy. In every chair sat a patient with an obvious physical disability. It was a sad sight.

Inside the Admitting Office, we went through the usual forms of insurance and responsibilities. The receptionist was completely absorbed in her paperwork when Mary asked, "How long is the program?

She looked up at Mary and said, "That all depends on him. It depends on how fast he wants to learn the new skills. It generally takes about eight weeks. Some patients take ..."

"Eight weeks!" I interrupted, looking at Mary.

Mary, trying to comfort me said, "Your fusion took three months—all of it in bed, and flat on your back. At least here you will be on your feet. You needn't worry about me. I will be able to handle things while you're gone. I know I can do it."

Mary held onto my hands and pressed them hard.

"You're not that far away, either. If I need any information, I can call you."

The last of the paperwork was finally completed. I signed on the dotted line and so did Mary. A staff member from the Pain Unit arrived. She cordially greeted both of us. Her prettiness perked up what was turning into a dull, painful day. Did Mary notice that my face reddened, and my eyes opened wider? It was difficult to keep it from her, but she said nothing.

"She can't be a nurse," I whispered to Mary. "She isn't wearing a uniform." She was dressed in a very casual way. We followed her out of the admittance office.

"You do have a wheelchair for my husband, don't you?" Mary asked.

"No, I don't," she answered, smiling all the while. "In the Pain Unit, we want the patients to become independent of their pain, no matter how severe it is. We don't want them to depend on aids."

To my surprise and exasperation, that meant walking. How could she expect that of me, in my condition at this moment? I was barely hanging on to my sanity because the pain was so intense. Mary carried the bags. She always carried the bags. I followed, bent over, dragging my painful left leg and carrying my pain.

Walking briskly and smiling all the time, the girl asked, in a friendly manner, "Where are you from?"

Mary answered, "We're from Salem."

"What a coincidence! I'm from Salem!" she answered.

It turned out that we had common acquaintances. That helped to take my mind off my pain.

Mary stopped, put the bags down for a moment, and asked, "Are you a nurse?"

"Absolutely," and then looking at her dress, she said, "The Pain Unit wants an impression of a community-like atmosphere, not of a hospital. They prefer a common dress. We have the option to wear or not to wear the hats."

We started walking again, our young nurse in the lead, and I stumbling along behind. Finally, we arrived at my room and she pointed at the bed closest to the door. "Another staff member will be in with more forms to fill out," she informed us. I fell on the bed and groaned.

Mary emptied my bags and stored my things, except for the cigarettes, in the drawers and closet. When I was finally able to pull myself up on the side of the bed—the pain had subsided a bit—I carefully stacked the cigarettes into an easily accessible area in the top drawer of the bedside table. Finding the best place to stack cigarettes had become a habit, due to the many times I'd been a patient. Reaching or groping for them wouldn't be a problem. My cigarettes attended to, I laid my sore body on the bed, while Mary began looking around the room. The mattress proved to be comfortable enough. It was firm, and there was a bed board under it.

While I was getting adjusted to the bed, Mary cried out with a hint of cynicism, "Ed, look at these rules and regulations." She held up a card. "This is going to be an interesting stay for you."

I sensed some glee in her words, and her spirits seem to lift a little. "Let me see them," I demanded.

"No! I'll read them to you."

"Let me read them. They belong to me."

Teasing she said, "No! I want to read them out loud." She walked over to the edge of the bed, sat at the far end, and began reading. "Each patient will have to make his or her bed every morning before breakfast." Then Mary laughingly added, "How are you going to manage that?"

"Make my own bed?" I said in disbelief.

She continued reading. "All patients are responsible for their own medication schedule."

I cut in. "I don't understand that one. Are they saying they are not going to bring my medication to me?"

"Yes, that's correct! You're going to have to get your own at the right times."

"That can't be. It's illegal." I rolled over onto my side and tried to reach for the plastic sheet of rules she held in her hands. The attempt aggravated my back. Quickly, I returned to a straight position on the bed.

Mary kept reading. "Oh My God!" she said. "Wait until you hear this one!"

"Quiet, Mary. Please." I attempted a whisper. "You're too loud. This is a hospital, remember? There are other patients here."

"I can't help it. This is beautiful. I can't believe it." She stared at me, grinning from ear to ear. "This is the best of all. Listen carefully now! It's written right here! Patients are not allowed in their beds after breakfast, or during any activity time. The same rule is in effect after dinner. When supper is over, a patient is free to do anything he wishes. These rules will be strictly adhered to." She read them slowly and deliberately.

"GIVE ME THAT CARD!" I demanded.

"Wow, I can't believe this!" She got up and walked toward the window, turned around, and said, "You are definitely not going to believe this. Every morning you have to walk the hallway on this floor. You will keep track of how many laps you have done. At breakfast, during medical rounds, the doctor will read your progress sheet."

At that moment, a knock on the door interrupted us, and a woman entered the room, smiling, and saying, "Hello, what's going on here?"

I assumed she was another nurse. She was dressed no differently than anyone else, so it was hard to tell. She was tall, wore glasses and had a nice smile. She was also very businesslike in her manner.

"My wife loves your rules and regulations. She's a sadist."

"Are those rules really true? Are they? Is that what Ed will have to abide by everyday?" Mary asked.

"Yeah, is that true?" I asked.

"Yes, and that's why I'm here," she said. "I'm a staff nurse." She spoke firmly, but not harshly. "I want you to read those rules and regulations very carefully and understand them. I also have this week's activities' schedule and some forms for itemizing your personal effects for our files. Be sure to familiarize yourself with the rules and make a note of your designated group." She carefully scrutinized us, looking back and forth from one to the other. I enjoyed looking at her smile. Then she continued. "At one o'clock there will be a community meeting. Everyone must attend this meeting, even staff personnel. Then at two o'clock your group meets with Charley for Psychomotor."

I wasn't listening to what she was saying. Instead, the discomforts I was experiencing while she spoke were distracting me. Was it the pain or the feeling that she was studying me? I couldn't tell.

Then I heard her say, "Mal, will be your guide. She is in your group, and after dinner she will come by to escort you to the meetings. She will be able to answer any questions that you have. Do you have any now?"

My pain, as bad as it had ever been, compelled me to whine, "Yes, right now my back is killing me, and I need to stay on my bed. It hurts so much I'm afraid that I'll even pass out right h ..."

Before I could finish, the nurse kindly but firmly said, "Look at me ... I understand." She walked over to my bed and looked straight down into my eyes, as if trying to convince me of her sincerity.

I avoided her eye contact.

"I can see you're in a lot of pain, but trust me. If you need to pass out that's okay too. This is the place to do it. This is a structured program to help you deal with your pain. If you follow the rules you will find relief, and a whole new world will open up to you. But first, you must learn to trust us."

Bewildered? No, shocked, by her tacit refusal to hear about my pain. My back hurt, and attention had always been given to that hurt by all the other nurses and doctors. She was trying to tell me my pain was no big deal and paid no attention to it. She paused waiting for a response. I gave none.

She continued, "So please, fill out the Personal Effects Form and study the schedule. That's it for now." She crossed her arms and said, "Welcome to the Pain Unit. You are very lucky to be here and we will help you." Then waggling her finger at me she said, "You'll see." Then she walked out of the room.

I was utterly astonished by what she had said. No one had ever talked to me that way before. I wondered what new world was opening up. "Boy, I hope I don't meet up with her again," I said to Mary.

"Oh Ed, I'm sorry," Mary said trying to comfort me. She approached the head of the bed and bent over me, supporting herself with both hands on the bed. She looked straight at me and said, "Ed, it'll be all right. Wait and see." Then she took my hand into hers.

"Forget the rules. Just keep lying down until someone else comes in. Maybe the pain will go away." She then pulled back, took both my hands in hers, and squeezed them saying, "I have to leave now. Just don't worry. It's going to be all right. Something here, in my heart, tells me that this is the place for you." Her eyes filled with tears. Here we were, once again, with another goodbye, another long separation, another leaving. Then she started to gather up her things.

I covered my emotions with sarcasm and anger and said, "Yeah, that's easy for you to say. I'm the one who's stuck here, not you. Make sure you don't forget the cigarettes when you come back." I rolled to the other side of the bed. At that moment, the same nurse came back into the room, without knocking. She had more orders, more directions, more information.

"Pardon me. I'm sorry to disturb you again," she said. "Did you bring a bathing suit and some outdoor clothes?"

I repeated, "A bathing suit and outdoor clothes? No! Was I supposed to?"

Surprised, she asked, "Weren't you told at the interview to bring them?"

"They said nothing about bringing clothes, nor did they tell me over the phone that I needed to bring anything other than pajamas."

"Oh, I'm sorry. You had better have some sent over. You're going to need them."

Mary's face fell. "I'll bring some tomorrow after school."

"Good," said the nurse, and then she left the room.

"Ed, I didn't expect to come back until Saturday." She sounded like Mary the martyr instead of Mary the placator. Once outsiders left, our true personalities and problems emerged. No longer was she pleasant and cooperative. She had become a "poor me" person.

Gruffly, I said, "Sorry. At least you won't have to bring any cigarettes. I'll still have plenty."

I got up from the bed, kissed and hugged her loosely, and walked to the door, where she said, "You don't have to walk me to the elevator."

In actuality, Mary wanted me to walk her to the elevator, but would never tell me so. She wanted me to offer on my own, and I couldn't do it. She dreaded parting with me. We kissed and hugged again, and I watched her walk down the hallway and disappear into the elevator. She turned back once and waved.

I returned to my bed, and struggled to raise it to the level of my buttocks. The bed had a crank and it was at an awkward level for me to turn. There, that height was the most comfortable for getting into bed. Now there would be no bending and no strain on my back. I reached for a cigarette and lit it, not thinking of Mary but of my cigarettes. How I would like to give them up!

For a moment, I reflected on an image of my brother lying in a hospital bed at home in his living room. On one side of the bed was his oxygen tank, hooked up to a breathing machine, near a table full of medicines. He was always clutching a rubber tube that was inserted through a permanent hole in his throat. He would tell us, in a hoarse voice, how the doctors used that hole for experiments for tracheotomy procedures.

On the other side of the bed, another table held his cigarettes and an ashtray was always filled with the butt-ends and ashes. A pitcher of water and cola was always there. He would take the tube out of his throat, turn off the machine, and light up a cigarette to inhale the smoke. When he exhaled, some of the smoke would come out of the hole in his throat. Seeing smoke coming out of his throat always stuck with me.

If I could train myself to see that image of my brother, lying in his bed with smoke coming out of the hole in his throat, I might be able to quit smoking myself. Stopping only when the last rites of the church were being administered wasn't my idea of successfully giving up cigarettes. I hoped never to get to that point. As I took a deep drag and inhaled every bit of it, another thought came to mind. Maybe if I wrote down a hundred times, "I'm going to quit smoking", those words would force my subconscious to allow me to quit. Not today, I had other things to think about. I would start tomorrow. I took another deep drag. I liked it. It was all I had left.

5

SECONDARY GAINS

I put out my cigarette and was just about ready to doze off when my roommate walked in. He was walking bent over as if looking for something on the floor. He got to his bed and I could see he was experiencing a lot of pain. He finally managed to lie down. He began taking deep breaths. He blurted out, "I hope you like this place better than I do. The food is terrible, tastes like nothing, no taste at all. My name is Jim."

Jim was average height, slim and obviously in great distress. His high forehead was covered with beads of perspiration, indicating his struggles with pain. His hair was shoulder length; he needed a haircut. His face carried a surly expression. His voice was almost a snarl. A growl. He wasn't friendly.

"What are you in for?" he asked.

"And I'm Ed." I answered, "I had four back operations: two lamanectomies, both fused at the same time, and the fusion torn down."

Jim groaned.

I asked, "How long have you been here?"

Jim answered disgustedly, "I've been here for two lousy weeks and my pain is as bad now, or even worse, than it was when I arrived."

"You don't feel any better after two weeks?" I was aghast! "Doesn't anything help you at all?"

Jim didn't answer that question, but instead snapped, "I need to shut my eyes for a few minutes. We have a community meeting starting shortly."

We stopped talking.

It was time to go to the meeting. He laboriously got out of bed. He asked me to follow him, which I did. We left, with me dragging my leg, and he bent over as if bowing.

We entered the meeting room. It was a large room. Twenty patients and a half dozen staff members all sitting in a huge circle took up the entire area. We found two empty chairs and sat in them. All eyes came upon me when someone said we have a new patient amongst us. I was introduced. With great effort I stood up to acknowledge the introduction and eased myself back down immediately as the others voiced their "hellos" and "welcomes".

The meeting was called to order. Minutes of the last meeting were read. Old business was dealt with and new business came up. The morning coffee duty was turned over to the next room for the following week.

Some complaints were aired. Someone wanted to know why he couldn't go home every weekend. It was answered with, "Your insurance company won't agree to it. They are reluctant to allow more than one home visit a month. They claim you're in a hospital, not a vacation resort."

All business was dealt with. What couldn't be resolved was put on hold until the next meeting when more information would be available. There was a short silence. No one had anything else to bring up.

Next on the agenda, a young man was introduced as a graduate of the Unit. He came forward and smiled at everyone. He was in his mid thirties and certainly looked sure of himself.

He spoke with the same assurance saying, "Give the Pain Unit a chance to work. When I first got here, I knew nothing about my pain. All I knew was that it hurt. It hurt bad. As I got into the program, I learned where my pain was coming from, how badly I was treating it, how I was coming across to others, and most importantly, how I used it for secondary gains.

"I never knew what the phrase 'secondary gains' meant. Now I do. As a result of what I learned, I want to share a true story about how your pain can trick you. I decided to take advantage of the State Rehabilitation Program. They will pay the expenses if you can pass all the tests required. I passed them. I decided to go back to school and was accepted at the University."

I listened to him with great interest. I didn't know about benefits for the disabled. I was learning something.

He continued, "Introduction to Psychology was one of my subjects. I became friendly with the professor. She was interested in the Pain Unit and had back problems herself, but refused to be operated on. With this in common, we became quite friendly—friendly enough to be invited to her home for dinner and her to mine. At her home she always talked about her mother-in-law and how every time the mother-in-law flew in a plane she always got into an accident. How many lawsuits she had against the airlines. How she does nothing to help her with the dinners or dishes or anything while she is visiting. She called her mother-in-law a fat slob.

"The professor invited me to participate in her research project called 'At What Age Level Does a Child Use Pain or Illness for Secondary Gains?' She said it wouldn't be difficult and that I would gain extra credits. We would only work on it once a week. That really appealed to me, so I signed up for it immediately."

Our speaker, the 'graduate,' kept my attention. He walked back and forth and eyed his audience. He had us right where he wanted us. Everyone was listening.

"Our intimacy grew as we shared our back problems and especially when I shared my knowledge of the Pain Unit. About halfway into the course, during the time we were preparing to interview five- to eight-year-olds, the professor was absent from her class. I remembered what she had said in the early part of that week. She said her mother-in-law was going to stay with her for the weekend. I immediately wondered if her mother-in-law had had another accident and the professor needed some assistance.

"The following Monday the professor was in class. I asked if her mother-in-law had come to visit? She said yes. Then I asked what had happened Friday? Did her mother-in-law have another accident? She said no, thank God! But, strangely enough, she herself had experienced severe back spasms and had to spend the remainder of the weekend in bed. That's why she couldn't come in Friday. Her poor husband had to do all the entertaining for his mother while she remained bedridden for the entire weekend.

"I asked when her back had started hurting and reminded her that all was fine last Thursday. She did recall feeling great that day. All the way home she had been in good spirits. I asked what happened. She thought for a moment, and told me the back pain had started Thursday evening when she'd stooped down to pick up a piece of paper. She tried to pick it up and couldn't. It seemed to be glued to the floor. Finally, after much struggling, she managed. When she straightened up, a terrible pain stabbed her in the lower back and began shooting down her legs. She went right to bed and her husband called the doctor."

I remembered the many times I had stooped to pick up something off the floor and felt that excruciating pain start in my back and shoot down my legs. My back, at that very moment, was feeling the same torture, and I hoped this meeting would end quickly. I forced myself to listen.

He continued, "Then I asked her if anything happened before she tried to pick up the paper? She said nothing really. There wasn't much going on. She was tired. However, her husband did ask her to pick up his parents at the airport before going to class Friday. He had to meet with a client and didn't want to cancel it. That's all she said. I asked her about that episode of picking up the paper. 'Did your husband mention wanting you to meet his parents at the airport before you stooped down?' She said, 'Yes. It was after that request. I picked up the paper, and that's when a sharp jolt of pain stabbed me in my back and exploded down my legs. It was so bad, I had to go to bed immediately. I got into bed and couldn't move. He called the doctor. The doctor prescribed some percodans, and insisted on bedrest for a few days.'

"Then, I asked her when did your in-laws leave? She told me they left on the Sunday morning flight. And when did your pain go away? Sunday night she said, and she felt great—so good, that she and her husband went out to dinner. She said those percodans worked very well.

"I began to analyze that situation for her, slyly counting off on my fingers. 'You were asked to pick up your in-laws and you developed a painful back. You didn't have to pick up your in-laws. Your husband did. You didn't have to cook or do the dishes. Your in-laws left Sunday morning and so did your pain. You went out to dinner pain free. Would you say you were in the act of using secondary gains?'

"I'll never forget the look on her face. She was devastated. She was using secondary gains and didn't know it.

"Our research project, by the way, did suggest that five year olds use anything they can for secondary gains."

I tried sorting out what he was trying to say. He made no sense to me. Bending over and then straightening up created excruciating pain in me many times. When she bent over, something happened to her back. So what did he mean? The in-laws went home. She felt better. All I could think of was the percodans she took. They got rid of the pain. That's why she felt better.

He continued, "The skills you will learn here are marvelous skills. Learn them well. Make them a part of your being. Then a whole new world will open up for you. I'm living proof of that. I have never felt as well as I do now.

"One last point," he continued. "The University has a North and South Campus. You have to cross a river to get to either Campus. I'm taking an Art Course at the South Campus. I don't take the bus. I walk. Whenever I go to the South Campus, I always get smiles from people coming towards me. What a wonderful feeling that is. I love seeing people smile at me. Thank you for listening."

Everyone clapped.

The meeting was over. A few people formed a line to congratulate him. Most were on their way to the next activity. I was in the line when a tap below my shoulder instinctively made me turn.

"Down here. Boy, you're tall. I only come up to your chest. I'm Mal, your guide," she said, and took a drag on her cigarette.

Her voice was hoarse, sounding like a male. Her hair was shoulder length. The plaid shirt and long gray pants she was wearing did nothing for her body. She looked like a little boy. She wore no makeup. And, the way she spoke conveyed a friendliness that made me comfortable.

Mal was also a patient in the Pain Clinic and had been assigned to me as a guide.

"I will take you to your next activity," she said. "It's mine, too. We're both in the same group."

I wanted to congratulate the graduate, but she said we were going to be late and had better leave now.

I followed Mal out of the room. Outside, Mal turned her head toward me and said, "We're due at psychomotor."

She must have known I was about to ask what that was.

"You don't have to ask? New patients always ask that question." She took another drag on her cigarette and continued, "Psychomotor is a therapy that deals with our emotions that show up in our body language."

"Body language? What's that?" I interrupted.

"I understand it's like acting," she answered. "Actors study it to make sure their bodies are doing what their words are saying. Your body language will tell the therapist whether you're angry. Your body will react to the conflicts into which he has manipulated you. These conflicts create body signs that he reads as anger. Then he will ask, 'Do you want to go good buddy and bad buddy?' If you want to go that route you pick someone in the room to play the parts. If you prefer not to, you don't. I'm not sure if this kind of therapy is helping me."

I said, "This is all very confusing to me. What's this 'good buddy and bad buddy'?"

She answered, "The good and bad buddy will accommodate you through the rest of 'the structure'."

"What structure?"

"The one that you chose."

Nothing was making any sense to me. I said to her, "I don't know what you mean. You're confusing me with 'body language, good buddy and bad buddy, and now, structure'. What are you building?"

She laughed, "We're not building anything. The 'structure' is a method you choose to get rid of your anger."

"Anger! I don't have any anger," I said with a nervous laugh. I was getting frustrated. I repeated what she said. "Get rid of your anger? I haven't the faintest idea of what you're talking about."

"That's O.K," she said. "I had trouble in the beginning, too. I still don't understand it well enough to explain it. Why don't you wait until our session is over? Maybe you'll understand it better by sitting through it."

We entered a room that seemed to be prepared for our group. Two mattresses were leaning against the left wall. A neatly folded blanket with a pillow on top of it was sitting on the edge of each mattress. A circle made up of nine chairs was set up in the center of the room. They were the cheap chairs found in all institutional settings. By the window was an overstuffed couch. It was the type that when you sat in it, you could see and talk through your knees. I began anticipating the difficulty I would have in trying to get out of it. A two-foot by three-foot section of one of the walls protruded and distorted the symmetry of the room. It came out of the center of the wall. I thought, "What a strange place to have a part of the wall jut out like that."

On the way in Mal continued, "What you must remember is that each one in our group has to take a turn and talk. We are allotted a half-hour. We say whatever we want, and do whatever we want. The only one who can interrupt is Charley. You'll like him. He's great. I kind of think it's a little weird because of some strange happenings."

We took a seat in the circle. I fidgeted in the chair and wondered what I was getting involved with.

"Let me tell you some things about Charley, our therapist," Mal said. "You'll like him. He's great, sweet, and kind, but he can be scary sometimes. He can manipulate you into discussing some thoughts that you ordinarily would never talk about. It can get too close for comfort, but it seems to be helpful. He digs right in and gets to the heart of your hidden conflicts. If we don't want to talk about our 'secrets' we don't have to. We have a choice. We can either ask everyone to leave, so that we can be alone with Charley, or end it right there."

Not long after we arrived, the other members of the group began trickling in. Charley and the two aides were among them. He walked towards my chair along with the two aides and introduced them as Kay and Agnes. They welcomed me with warm smiles and a touching hello. Charley was short, with red hair and a strawberry blonde beard. Every hair follicle on his face was part of his beard. Just the nose, upper cheekbone and eyes were free from hair. He, too, had a comforting appeal to his voice.

As the others entered, they greeted me with a variety of welcomes ranging from "Hi", to "Welcome aboard" to

"You'll find this place to be helpful" to "You better leave before it's too late."

At the latter, Mal said gruffly to the group, "Be quiet, don't scare the guy."

The door was about to be closed when a woman, who was a little on the heavy side, barged in. She took no notice of me, or of anyone else for that matter. She stomped to an empty chair and before sitting down started spewing, "That bastard! Would you believe it? I just got through talking to him over the phone. He said he had to work last night, and that's why he couldn't come to visit me. He's lying! I know he is!"

I looked at the others in the circle. They were all getting themselves comfortable in their chairs. No one except Charley was watching her very closely.

She continued, "That bastard! The son-of-a-bitch is fucking around with another woman! I know he is! He never wants to do anything with me!"

I felt myself starting to blush. I sat up straight in my chair and began to listen. It was okay for men to curse, but I wasn't comfortable when a woman did it.

Someone said, "Sounds like you're ready for the blanket."

The woman answered sarcastically, "I don't want the god damn blanket!"

The blanket? I sat up straighter and listened harder. Why did they mention a blanket? It wasn't cold. She certainly wasn't going to nap was she? I was starting to feel confused and uncomfortable.

"You all know what happened last week! He was here!" she said with tears running down her cheek. "You saw how he wouldn't comfort me when I cried. He never tries to make me feel good."

I wondered if she cried often, like my wife.

"He wanted me to leave the Pain Unit. Remember? He said the Pain Unit wasn't doing anything for me except filling me up with crazy ideas."

A patient got up, walked over, and gave her a Kleenex. She took it and wiped her eyes. The patient gently patted her shoulder saying, "It's okay. It's okay, Claudia."

She began ranting again. "That fucking bastard! He's always working late at night, but his paychecks don't know it. My sister had to ask me who the bimbo was he's been out with lately! While I'm in here!"

I felt more blood flushing into my face as my body shrank into the chair. I hoped no one noticed my blushing. Her vulgarity struck an uneasy chord throughout my being. But it was funny how my back had stopped aching during this tirade.

"Claudia, do you want the blanket?" It was Charley again.

"NO! I don't want the damn thing!"

The veins in her neck were tightening and grew into strands like rope under her skin. Her eyes grew wide and glaring and cast no doubt in my mind that she was falling into some sort of a diatribe. Her eyes, her mouth, her forehead, her entire face turned into ugliness. Her body reacted to whatever she was experiencing with stony rigidity. I had never seen anything like it and didn't know if I wanted to see it now.

My eyes searched the others in the circle. I found no one who seemed concerned. Didn't they care? It seemed like I was the only one affected, and I didn't know what to do. What if she cracked? What would happen then? There were no answers or comfort in the faces of the others. They just sat there, letting it happen.

Claudia continued in her ugliness and spat out, "Today he called and told me that my daughter—not his of course—is smoking pot. He saw the hand-rolled cigarettes when her purse fell to the floor and spilled. He grabbed the cigarettes and asked her what they were. She told him that she was saving them for a friend. Then he had the nerve to ask me what I was going to do about it? How the fuck can I do anything about it? I'm in here!"

My mind cringed with her constant vulgarity. Then I thought about what she'd said.

The answer her daughter gave about saving the cigarettes for a friend was too familiar. My daughter had used the same words.

"Do you want the blanket?" Charley asked again. It almost sounded as if he was pleading with her to take it.

"No!" she yelled.

It seemed that she didn't really mean it.

He repeated the question, "Claudia, I'm offering you the blanket?"

It still seemed like a plea for her to take it.

"Do you want to be restrained?" This time his voice carried a soothing type of energy, not only to her but to me, too. It appeared that he knew it would be good for her, but why, was beyond my understanding.

"All right! All right! I'll do it. Just leave me alone!"

Kay and Agnes got up quickly and walked over to the mattresses.

Mal's hoarse, cigarette-smoking voice, sounding like gravel falling, tried to whisper in my ear, "Kay and Agnes are Charley's designated henchmen. They're always with him and always seem to know what to do at the right time. They're great. You'll see. Watch what they do now."

Agnes took the pillow and blanket, then walked back to the circle, placing them on her chair. She went back, and with Kay, they both brought the mattresses, one at a time, into the center of the circle. They placed them one on top of the other. Then Agnes placed a pillow on the mattresses while Kay held on to the blanket. Claudia got up. She walked over to the mattresses and stared at them. After a moment, she got down and lay on them, placing the pillow under her head.

"Are you sure you want to go through with this?" Charley's voice was kind and caring. Soothing. It came across like some kind of healing energy.

She answered with a soft, "Yes."

"Okay," Charley said. He got up, walked over to the mattresses and stopped.

I watched and listened to what was going on, and could hardly believe what was happening. My anxiety was ready to explode. Why was she lying on the mattress? What was that blanket for? My mind had thought back at some weird stories I had read about and seen at movies. There was something just as strange happening here, at this moment, and it was real.

Claudia was so tense her body looked as if it was ready to snap and break into little pieces. I watched every move very carefully and checked to see where the door was, in case I felt it necessary to run. Something was going to happen. There was no question in my mind about that. The desire to stay and see it was fighting with the desire to leave and forget about it. Both feelings increased the anxiety inside of me.

Everyone got up and circled Claudia's body, except me. I sat there in my chair, not knowing what to do, or if I wanted to do it.

"Okay, spread the blanket over her," Charley ordered.

Kay unfolded the blanket on top of Claudia, leaving only her head exposed. The others got down onto the floor. Some squatted. Some kneeled, and some just bent over. All seven people held the edge of the blanket and pulled it tightly over Claudia.

"Ed, come on over and take hold of the blanket," Charley invited.

The sound of his voice was strangely comforting. It was this comfort that gave me the desire to be a part of whatever was going on. It almost felt safe. I got up, walked over, and took hold of the blanket at Claudia's feet. She was starting to move as I tried to get a comfortable grip on the blanket.

Charley instructed, "Make sure you have a good grip on the blanket. We don't want to lose it. Most important, when she starts, make sure you're pulling it with a downward motion. She must not break out." Charley looked at the body under the blanket and said, "I can see you're ready."

She had already started to struggle to get out from underneath the blanket. Gradually her struggle increased, forcing me to tighten my grip to hold her in place. The others tightened their grips as well. This was unbelievable! This woman agreed to be forcibly held down on the mattresses with a blanket. "FOR WHAT REASON?" I kept asking myself. Her struggle turned into a writhing, and it became more difficult to hold her down. I was holding so tightly that my back began to complain, with a sharp burst of pain shooting in every direction.

Agnes was saying to Claudia, "You're doing fine. Squirm out of it. You have a lot of energy to get rid of. That's it. Keep squirming."

It seemed as if Agnes was accommodating her, prodding her to go on. As Agnes spoke, Claudia would wriggle even harder. The more Agnes accommodated, the more violent Claudia's squirming energy became under that blanket. We had to use more energy to hold her down. I wondered how long we could keep that kind of balance.

She was like a volcano erupting. The tighter my hold on the blanket became the more pain I felt in my back. Trying to hold down that blanket was like trying to hold down a fish out of water. She was going to break through. I was afraid that she would break through at my end. GOD! I prayed. Stop this nonsense! The pain in my back was radiating down my legs and up into my shoulders. It seemed like hours had passed, and we were still struggling to hold Claudia down.

My energy ran out. I barely held onto the blanket, leaving it up to the others.

She began to tire and eased up on her wriggling, but Kay was asking for more. "Get it all out Claudia. Get every bit of it out." Claudia didn't have enough energy to continue, and she slowly brought her body to rest under the blanket.

I let go of the blanket, got up with great effort, sat on my chair, and stared at the blanket with Claudia under it. An uncontrolled tremble shook my body. It only lasted for a second. Was this all for real, or would I wake up any moment now? It was real. The most striking part of it all was what was happening to her. The tightness and the veins in her neck and face were disappearing. The ugliness that her face had assumed was no longer there. As her face relaxed, so did her body. She seemed to be much prettier than before. Her frown was gone. She took on a special beauty. This woman was not ugly after all.

"How do you feel?" Charley asked.

Her voice was weak but clear as she said, "I feel fine. I feel completely relaxed. I feel so good." She seemed to mean everything she said. Her voice became just as beautiful as her face. What a remarkable change had occurred here!

It was all over. Claudia got up and slowly went to her seat as if nothing had ever happened. My mind tried to sort out what my eyes, ears and hands had seen, heard and felt.

"Who wants to be next?" Charley asked.

6

RELEASING ANGER

I looked at the other patients and pleaded silently with my eyes. No, not me. Please …Oh, God, no, not me. I can't do that. Never. I wasn't ready for this at all. I think Charley knew it, too. His eyes left me and they swept around the room. No one answered his call.

Charley looked toward Mal and asked, "Mal, how did your weekend go at home?"

My guide was forced into her turn. She had no choice. As she spoke, severe pain began shooting down my legs. She was saying something about her female friend who was living with her. The more she talked about her friend, the more pain I began to feel. It was growing intolerable. I was afraid to get up for fear of interrupting. I also didn't want anyone to notice me. I felt like a snake wiggling and wriggling in my chair. The more I tried not to be noticed, the more tense I became. I was becoming completely racked with pain. I had to get up. Finally, the pain got so bad that I didn't care about interrupting. I walked around the back of the chairs and around the room trying to shake off the pain. The more Mal spoke the worse I got. Everything she said was about her girlfriend who was living with her, as if they were married. All I could think of was my percodans. How I wished I had some!

Mal was having no easy time of it either. She was rubbing her arms. She would switch from one to the other, rubbing fiercely, talking all the while.

On the far wall of the room, there was a niche that was in line with Mal's seat. I made my way slowly into it and tried to hide there. I was hiding from the vibes of pain that seemed to be coming my way from Mal. It was no use. Hiding didn't help. The pain was excruciating. I was pressing my body as far into that niche as I could. It didn't keep the pain out. The pain got worse. I had no idea what I was doing. I was losing my mind.

Charley's eyes were searching both of us. He watched every thing we were doing. Mal was hurting as much as I was, but she had to stay in the circle.

"Time's up," Charley announced without any warning, "We'll continue this next time."

Reluctantly, I got back to my chair. Charley watched my every move. As I walked the sharp pains began leveling off. I eased my body into the chair. Mal was all done, and she seemed to be more comfortable.

Charley spoke, "Ed, you have just been introduced to psychomotor. It wasn't planned that way. Your introduction to Claudia and the releasing of her anger was obviously difficult for you. Why your pain acted up at the same time Mal spoke, and the pain in her arm reacted in the same way as yours, can't be explained at this moment. I need to know more about you. I don't think it would be appropriate at this time to subject you to a turn. You've had enough for your first day at the Pain Unit. If you have any questions, I will try to answer them for you. In any case, welcome to psychomotor."

"Thanks," I said with a sigh of relief, and added, "I hope my pain doesn't continue to flare up every time Mal speaks." I allowed myself to wallow in the relief of not having to take a turn.

"Charley, I'm in a turmoil over what I think was anger coming from Claudia while she was trapped in the blanket. I'm a Catholic and to get angry like that is a sin. I would have to tell that sin in the confessional."

Charley answered, "First of all, know this. I, too, am a Catholic. When you release anger at a person, and the anger hurts that person, it's a sin. Releasing anger—the way you will learn it here—instead of repressing it, is a helpful skill to prevent illnesses. That is not a sin. Trust me, Ed, it's not a sin. What you've witnessed here is called a 'structure'. A structure is a method for releasing all that pent up anger inside of you. Remember the physical changes that occurred during the episode? Claudia was angry, ready to explode. Now she's relaxed, able to deal with anything that comes her way. Claudia dealt with her anger and released it upon an inanimate, harmless object. She didn't hurt anyone, nor did she hurt herself. By releasing her anger, Claudia was strengthening her ability to deal with experiences of that kind. The only other alternative is to repress the anger and that would be damaging to Claudia's health. You'll find, as we continue with this structure, the blanket isn't the only way to deal with anger. There are other releases."

"This is scary," I interrupted.

"Ed," Charley continued, "if Claudia had repressed her anger, it would have come back to haunt her, creating more pain and anxiety within her. That anxiety would lead to more anger, and the vicious circle would start all over again."

"If I were somewhere else and decided I needed to release my anger, wouldn't my rage be beating up on someone?" I asked.

"No!" said Charley. "Here, you will learn to be in complete control of your anger. If you weren't in control of yourself, you wouldn't be here. You would be in another kind of hospital. As you progress in the program, you'll find other ways that can be useful to deal with your anger."

He looked straight into my eyes. I avoided them. There was something about the way he spoke. His voice, his choice of words, and his capacity to listen to every word I used gave me a great deal of comfort. It was easy to listen to him and to believe whatever he said. I knew he was helping me.

"Okay," Charley said. "Our time is up. I'll see you all next time."

He got up, stretched his entire body, then walked around the room while Mal, the other patients, and I exited. Charley, Kay, and Agnes remained. On the way out I asked Mal, "What did you think of the anger bit?"

Before she could answer, a couple of the patients hollered out, "See you at supper with your new boyfriend."

Mal laughed. The others just went on their way.

"To answer your question, I've done it. It always felt good. The blanket is Claudia's favorite. She has good reasons to be angry. I'm sure she'll be getting a divorce. Her husband is just no good."

"You mean she's done this before?"

"Oh yes, many times," she answered. "But I prefer the pool. Wow, can I ever beat and kick that water, and it feels so good."

"Beat and kick the water?"

"Yeah. The water helps to wash away the rotten feelings from anger."

"I don't know about all this stuff. I'm perplexed. I don't know if I can do all that."

"Ed, I was a lot worse than I am now. I have a lot of anger inside of me, and I know that the pain in both my wrists are part of my pent up anger. You, too, will find that out. Right now everything is confusing. And, why not? How can anyone prepare you for this, especially, your first day. You have to experience it."

"I guess you're right."

"It's after five o'clock, and time for meds. After meds is supper. I'll take you to meds. Then give me a few minutes to wash up for supper, and we'll go to the dining room. Okay?"

"That's fine with me. I need a nap. I need to relax."

At the nurses' station I was introduced to the distribution of medication. The nurse gave me two percodans, checked my name off the list, and made sure I took them while she watched. She also informed me that at the morning medical rounds the doctor would discuss my medication. Whatever he decided on it would be my responsibility to get them at the specified times.

I went to my room. My roommate was asleep. I thought, that's what I'd like to be doing right now. I fell on my bed. Come on, percodans, come on. Start working.

7

ICE MASSAGE

What a day! I hadn't been that busy and that tired for two years. No wonder my back hurt so much! I could feel the percodans working and finally fell asleep. When I woke, some time later, I noticed Jim had left. I didn't really care. I needed to be alone for a while. I just lay there trying to sort out the events of the day.

Jim came in carrying a newspaper. He told me what to do if I wanted to buy one every day. Since I was addicted to the comics and crossword puzzles, I indeed wanted one.

He handed me a section and with a sneer in his voice said, "I heard you had quite a jolt at that weirdo psychomotor." He had an unpleasant smile on his face.

"Yes, I've never seen anything like that," I agreed.

"Did you have a turn? Did they put you through the paces?"

"No. Charley thought I'd had enough, so he didn't ask me to take one."

"You're lucky," he grumbled. "I wish Charley would leave me alone." With that, he began to read his paper.

I started to read the section he'd given me. I must have fallen asleep again while reading and was startled when I was shaken by an aide. She was carrying a plastic container and had towels draped over her arms and shoulder.

"Hi. My name is Alice, and I know you're Ed. Am I right?" she asked. Her face was lovely and her smile was warming and pleasant to see.

"Yes," I answered, still trying to put my mind in focus. Percodans sometimes leave me feeling woozy.

"It's time for your ice massage!"

I looked over at Jim and waited for him to say something, since I didn't know what she was talking about.

Alice beat him to it and said, "Every night at about this time, you'll get an ice massage."

"An ice massage?" I repeated. "What's an ice massage?"

"Yeah!" Jim snorted. "She's the coldest person in the world. All she wants to do is torture you with that cake of ice."

Jim's disposition was not very pleasant at all.

"Now, Jim ..."

He interrupted, "Notice! She keeps it hidden! She wraps it in her little plastic box of tricks. Some day I would like to give her an ice massage and see how she likes it."

I wanted to join in the repartee that seemed to be going back and forth, but didn't know what an ice massage was, and had to wait to find out.

"Jim, I'm going to do you first. Okay?" Alice asked.

"Yeah, okay."

"Good, and you won't mind if I enjoy every bit of it? In fact," Alice grinned, "I picked the coldest piece of ice, just for you."

I laughed at that. Alice walked over to Jim's bed and asked if he minded leaving the curtain open, so that I could see what was going on.

He agreed and blurted, "Please do! Let him watch how you torture me with that ice. Then I'll be able to use him as a witness when I take you to court for cruelty to a patient."

She smiled. He removed his shirt and t-shirt, lowered his pants to the top of his buttocks, and lay on his stomach. I watched. Alice tucked towels along the sides of Jim's back. Then she folded one and placed it over his buttocks, tucking an end inside his pants. She unwrapped a face cloth that hid a large piece of ice. She began to apply the ice to the lower part of Jim's back, and to every place he said he had pain. The water from the melting ice rolled onto the towels that were protecting his bed and pants from getting wet

"It's numb! You can stop now. It's numb," he snarled, a few seconds later.

I waited to see what that meant.

Alice took another towel and wiped the wetness from his back. She cupped each hand and began to beat, with one hand then the other, in a rhythmic fashion, over the small of his back. Each beat had an echoing slapping sound to it. Jim lay there motionless, allowing her to continue the massage to its end.

I watched the ice massage being given and wondered how that could possibly help me. The slapping on the iced area, what can that possibly do for me other than hurt me more?

Alice walked over to my bed and said, "Now, It's your turn."

"Must I? I really don't want to."

"Yes! You must!"

"That didn't look like fun to me! It looks more like you'll be creating more pain."

"Turn over and prepare your back." She was still smiling at me, but quite firm about what she intended to do. "You will get a lot of relief from this massage. You'll see." She spoke with a convincing comforting tone.

Since I had no choice, I turned over and did what she asked. When I was all prepared, and waiting, she applied it. I felt my entire body tighten right up, but I did get some immediate relief as the icy cold numbed away the pain.

Again Alice explained each step of the massage. While rubbing the painful areas, she asked me to let her know when the areas became numb.

"I'm not sure what the numbness should feel like. How long should it take?" I asked.

Alice answered, "It only takes a few seconds, and that depends on how much tolerance you have. You shouldn't be able to feel anything now. I'm going to pinch you. Can you feel that?"

"No, I can't."

"That means it's numb. You will get used to it and know exactly when it is numb." Alice began the rhythmic beating.

"Why do you do that? I hear the slapping, but I don't feel anything."

"Good. That's really a good sign," Alice said. "The beating is diverting blood from its usual flow to the painful areas."

A moan came from me. I felt no pain.

Alice continued, "There, its healing qualities will go to work to bring relief, albeit for a short time. But, something is better than nothing."

I expected to feel the strikes when she started the slapping. There was hardly any feeling to them at all. I could have let her go on all night, but it abruptly came to an end.

"There, how was that?" Alice asked.

"Just great!" I answered, nearly swooning. "It really felt soothing. What a beautiful invention! Whose idea was that? And you're going to do this every night?"

"Yes! Every night, and also in the morning, before the seven o'clock shift comes on." With that, Alice gathered the towels and bid us goodnight. It was like something beautiful had just left the room.

"Seems like you found a new customer for your cold tortures," Jim said, as Alice walked out of the room smiling.

I just lay there and wallowed in the pain-free state Alice had created. I didn't dare move, for fear it would all come back. I enjoyed every short minute of it.

Finally, I got up. I knew I had to get up some time. The moment I moved, all the pain rushed in, finding its usual areas to settle in. It seemed like it rushed to get back to those areas, to let me know that this stuff wasn't going to work. The areas that had been free from pain for that short period of time now seemed to hurt more than ever. In despair, I thought to myself, was it all worth it? If it becomes worse after the massage, what good is it? How do I deal with this?

I made myself go down the hall for my ten o'clock medication. I came back and went to bed. I tried to sleep, but the entire day's events passed by in blocks of thoughts. This was the busiest day I had ever had since this pain of mine became a permanent companion. I hate it. I hate all of it. I don't want to be here. I've suffered enough. Tears came and I let them roll.

8

BODY MASSAGE

At nine o'clock every morning except Sundays, I had a body massage scheduled. This morning I was waiting for Mal, my guide. She was to accompany me on my way to the massage room. I limped out into the hallway and leaned against the wall. I could see Mal walking towards me. She was holding on to her elbows.

"Hi, Ed. Good morning," Mal said, as she continued to rub her elbows back and forth.

"What's good about it? I hurt all over," I retorted, while leaning heavily against the wall favoring my bad leg. "My worse time is the first thing in the morning. I don't find anything good about this morning. My leg hurts so much I sometimes wish they would cut it off."

"Ed, don't say that." There was a warning tone in her voice. "One of the patients who used to be here had lost an arm. He couldn't stand the pain where there was no arm. Not a good idea, Ed."

"Are you kidding me? He had pain where there was no arm?" I asked. "I can't believe that."

"No, I'm not kidding," Mal said. "He lost his arm, and they call it a phantom limb."

"Oh God," I groaned.

Together we walked toward the massage room. We were both miserable, and neither of us felt like talking very much. She was rubbing her elbows and I was bent over, always conscious of my enflamed left leg. Finally I had to ask, "Why do you keep rubbing your elbows."

Mal answered, "I was in an accident and both arms, from the wrist to the elbows, were crushed. The doctors are trying to fuse the crushed bones into healthy ones. It's not working. Both are always hurting. I don't understand why my elbows have to hurt. Sometimes the pain shoots up into my shoulders. Then I'm in real trouble."

"That is rough," I said.

We didn't talk anymore. I thought of my upcoming massage, wondering if it was going to be the same as others I had received in hospitals. All they did was rub the skin a little with alcohol and let it dry. Only occasionally was the rub really any good.

We entered a large room containing three individually curtained sections. Three chairs sat against the windowed wall, and each faced an aqua-colored section. One area had its curtain drawn open. Partially hidden by the curtain stood the massage table. The table almost filled the area, leaving little room around it for work purposes.

"Lena," Mal called out in her raspy, cigarette voice.

There was no answer.

"Lena!" she repeated, louder this time. "Where are you? Ed's here for his massage!

A muffled voice from a distance answered, "Thank you, Mal! I'll be ready in a minute!"

The sound, coming from behind the far curtain, had an appealing tone and accent to it. It was foreign, but familiar.

Mal left, saying goodbye to the voice and then to me.

Again with that foreign accent I heard, "Ed!" It was a lovely sound.

"Yes!" I answered.

"Strip to your shorts and put your clothes on the chair."

I was suddenly shy about removing my clothes. I didn't know what to do. I just stood there.

She continued with, "Then go and lie face down on the empty table. You will see a towel there. Draw it over your shorts.

I was embarrassed as she spoke, but her accent kept me wondering to which country it belonged. It was haunting me. I was too reticent to ask her.

I did as she said and then sat on the narrow table, wondering how to lie down without creating more pain. I tried to lift my legs, and at the same time, rest an elbow on the table. Bursts of pain, shot down from the small of my back through both legs. I lay there for a moment, on my side, then slowly turned on to my stomach. Every inch of the turn became sheer agony. I finally made it on to my stomach and began to breathe heavily. Next, I had to deal with my arms. Where would I put them? The table was too narrow to put them along my sides. There was no room left. I folded my arms over my head and rested on them. While I was resting and waiting, I kept wondering where she was from. Her accent was definitely not American.

With my head on my arms, all I could see was the floor. I heard a clatter. It mingled with the ruffling of the curtain.

Wooden shoes came into view. A sculptor couldn't have shaped those ankles any better. They seemed very happy in their place. The wooden shoes loosely supporting them not only added to their beauty, but seemed proud to have them. The calves above the ankles were as perfect as anyone could find. Then they disappeared.

"You must place your arms down along your sides." Her heavenly accent floated out at me. "I don't want your head to cut off the blood circulating in your arms."

I couldn't raise my head to see her. There was that mysterious accent again. What country did it come from? I knew I'd heard it many times before. Her sabots made me think she might be Dutch or Norwegian. She kept walking around the table.

Again, her ankles came into view, distracting me. I just stared at them and forgot about the accent.

"Did you hear me?" she asked.

If only I were an artist, then those ankles and calves would be captured forever in a drawing. I knew the proportions would probably match the rest of the body in the same exquisite way.

"Yes, I hear you!"

I moved my arms to the side of my body. They slipped off. My nervous laugh came from somewhere deep inside me. "See! I'm too big for the table!" I exclaimed. "I have trouble keeping my arms along my sides."

"I guess you will have to let them hang there for now," she said.

My eyes picked up the ankles and calves again, and the delight returned. I grasped the legs of the massage table and felt more comfortable for a while. She applied warm oil to my back and legs. That felt good. The warmth of the oil penetrated deeply.

"My name is Lena, and I know you're Ed. I am assigned to you as your masseuse and counselor."

Her accent had a wonderful ring to it. It was driving me crazy. I heard myself ask, "What kind of accent is that?" My tongue twisted the words out of my mouth.

Lena laughed, "It's Swedish. I was born in Sweden."

I breathed a sigh of relief and said, "That's right! I knew it was familiar."

"Oh, you have been to Sweden?"

"No!" I said, clearing my throat, "No! I have never been to Sweden, but I just saw a movie about World War II. It was filmed in Sweden. They all spoke with your accent. I do dream of going there, and my favorite car is a Volvo."

"Then we must get rid of your pain so that you can go to Sweden. I will help you do that."

"Oh, if only you could do that. If only you could," I groaned, more to myself than to Lena.

"Now, you must let me explain what will happen as I massage."

Her voice was lulling and soothing. I could only see the white hem of her skirt. It was hanging just below her knee. Now that I knew where her accent came from, I wondered if she looked like Inga Stevens, Elke Sommers, or Liv Ullman?

Lena said, "I will be doing therapeutic massages on your back and legs. With your help, I'll try to break up all the knots that are set in your back. We call them tension knots."

"I have knots in my back? How come no one else noticed them?"

"I'm a masseuse. It's my job to know."

"How long will it take?" I asked.

"It doesn't happen in a day. It takes a while. How long is entirely up to you."

There it was again, I thought. It was up to me. It's always up to me! I wished I could understand why they kept saying that. Irritation was beginning to set in. If it were up to me I wouldn't have the pain. I would have gotten rid of it a long time ago.

Lena continued, "I'm using a special oil made from coconuts that doesn't dry out. It's very good for your skin. I'll wipe it off with alcohol when I'm through. That way, it won't stain your clothes."

She began applying the oil for the second time.

"That oil feels good," I said, as she applied it to my legs and back.

"Good."

When she was all done oiling me, she walked over to a table and placed the bottle of oil on it. Each step with those ankles and calves mesmerized me.

Lena returned and said, "Now, I will start the massage from the heal of your right leg. Then I will switch to your left leg. I want you to concentrate on it."

She began to stroke upwards, from the heel.

"What I want you to do is to concentrate on the flow of my hands. I will be pushing upwards. I want you to imagine your blood in your veins being pushed with my hands. Your blood flows in that direction. Every time my hands push up on your legs, try to imagine the flow of your blood being helped along its way."

"I can't see any blood. Nothing wants to come to my mind except how good it feels. What a wonderful feeling."

"I know it is difficult to do for the first time, but you will learn to do it," she said.

When she got to the small of my back, her hands spread out and up to the ends of my shoulders, all in one stroke. She started again and stopped at the base of my skull. I could hear her exhale each time she made a stroke. Each stroke sent me into heaven. I had never felt anything like it before. She repeated the strokes. I took in every one. Her rubbing and kneading were hypnotic. I was feeling true ecstasy. No other massage has ever felt like this.

"If you should feel any pain from my massage, let me know and I'll ease up."

If she were hurting me I would never tell.

Lena explained, "I'll work hard on those tension spots, but I won't know if I am hurting you unless you tell me. Your limits of pain are only known to you. I don't know how much pain you can tolerate. Understand?"

"Yes," I said, in a thick, guttural sound. At the same time that I was trying to do as she wished, I was also trying to get a glimpse of this lovely person. The position I was in and the area she was working on just wouldn't allow me to see her entire body. I still had to settle for her ankles and calves. I didn't mind that at all! My state of mind was becoming euphoric.

"Are there a lot of knots in my back?" I asked, my voice still in thick with pleasure.

"I'm afraid your entire back is knotted. It's like a washboard."

How could my back be like that? I asked myself. "I don't know what you mean by a washboard." I thought of my mother and that rough board she used while laundering clothes for her eight children.

"Give me your hand, and I will let you feel the knots."

I obeyed, but I was in a terribly awkward position to really feel what she was trying to explain. I managed to touch just the edge of my back.

"Do you feel that hard spot there?"

"Oh! That!" I lied. I couldn't feel a thing. Why did I do that? Why did I "yes" everyone? Some day I will stop! I screamed to myself. Somehow I knew she sensed what I was thinking.

"As we get more and more involved, you'll know exactly what I mean," Lena said.

The way she said it was comforting. She warmed the oil in her hand before spreading it once again over my back, pushing upward. I could feel her hand helping my blood flow in that direction. The strokes seemed to be timed with her breathing. The effects excited me, sending soothing delights throughout my body. I had heard that the Swedish massages were wonderful to experience. Now, I was getting the real thing. She continued, and I was driven into deeper ecstasy. She asked if she were hurting me. If she was, the pain wasn't getting through to my brain. I lay there, enjoying every movement of her hands.

Her hands moved down to my legs. They had never been massaged. It was almost too much to believe. Pangs of pleasure ran through me. Why had it taken so long to find something like this? My mind flew in all directions. The ecstatic state created fantasies about all the beautiful places I had always wanted to go. She was sending me to all of them, and I never wanted to come back. Maybe she could teach me how to do it and apply it to Mary, so she could share the delights with me. I lay there and let it all pass through me.

All too soon she said, "You are going to feel some alcohol on your back. It will feel very cold." She was right. The cold quickly brought me back to reality.

Lena warned, "You may get up now, but not too quickly. Be very slow in getting up. Too fast and you will get dizzy."

The small, narrow table, the large man, the pain, and fear of falling, made my efforts to sit upright awkward and fumbling. After a few gyrating moments, I was able to rest limply on the edge of the table. I stared at her. Being able to see all of her would solve my mystery. She didn't disappoint me.

"Is there something the matter? You're staring at me."

My face turned red. I was embarrassed. With an apology I explained that I hadn't been able to see what the rest of her looked like while I was lying on the table. I told her I'd been right about her. She was attractive, and I just wanted to look at all of her. I thanked her for the massage and added that it had sent me into a state of ecstasy.

She smiled and thanked me.

"Tomorrow, hurry up and come," I blurted. "Do you give seconds?"

She laughed. "Only one massage to a customer, Ed. But thanks for the nice thoughts."

Lena told me that my legs were going to feel odd when I attempted to stand up on the floor. She said I should wait a moment before attempting to walk.

I slid off the table and tried to steady my legs, but couldn't. They felt odd and rubbery. The fear of falling made a chill run down my spine as I began to crumble. Lena instinctively grabbed me, as if she had done it many times before. Sitting on the table and shaking my legs to get their strength back, I tried again, but this time very slowly. I managed to steady myself, even though it took a few moments for me to realize the floor was under my feet. When my legs felt steady, they were finally committed to walking. I thanked her again and slowly walked out.

9

POOL THERAPY

I lit a cigarette and walked to my room feeling as light as a feather. What an experience my body was enjoying, like walking on air! As soon as I got to my room, reality struck me. The pain in my back suddenly shot down through my legs and into my toes. If only there was a hole in those toes! Then the pain could shoot right out of them, instead of returning to repeat its torture.

I went to the supply room and found the hydroculators. A set of directions was taped to the wall above them. I followed the directions carefully to prevent any burns. I spread out three towels, one on top of the other, on a table. With a slight bending of my body, I retrieved the hydroculator from the heater and placed it on top of the towels. I folded the towels' sides on top to enclose it. Then, off I went to my room, carrying it as if it were a tray.

Back in my room, I placed the hot pack in the center of the bed. More pain grabbed my spine and shot down through my legs. Was it the bending that was creating this pain I wondered? Could such an easy task exacerbate the hurt more than before? I had done nothing difficult.

I positioned the small of my back on the center of the hotpack and waited for the heat to do its work. It seemed like forever before the heat penetrated. Its slow effect and my need for a quick relief was vexing. It took more than five minutes for the real heat to settle in. Finally it came. More and more of it came. Was it too hot? No. It could never be too hot for me. At its peak the heat seemed to devour my pain. After ten minutes, its effect began dissipating. As it decreased, the pain returned. Damn! Again reality took control over wishful thinking.

A quick glance at my watch indicated pool time was beginning. I did not have a bathing suit, but I had to be there, whether or not I participated in the pool exercises.

Mal entered the room and asked, "Are you ready for the pool?"

"Kind of," I answered. "I don't have a bathing suit. My wife will bring one tonight. What will I do?"

"I know there are some extra suits for us in the ladies' locker room," she answered. "There must be some extra suits in the men's." Her head tipped slightly downward. She looked at the lower half of my body. "You may have difficulty in finding one that'll fit. That could be a problem." She smiled.

I looked at my protruding stomach. "Yes, I know what you mean."

We left my room, and joined the other patients going to the pool. We stopped at the entrance to the men's dressing room.

"Here it is," Mal said. "Wish you luck!" She headed for the ladies' room.

Inside the dressing room, I found individual lockers with keys that were attached to stretchable rings. They would fit any wrist or ankle.

All the conveniences were in the room, including a special shampoo and a body lotion. There was a sign on a locker next to the towel rack. It read, "bathing suits". I found one that showed some promise, and with a lot of effort, changed into it. It became a chore to hold my stomach in all the time, but I managed, and reluctantly followed the others to the pool.

The pool was not very big. It had stairs, with a railing on either side for easy access and exit. It also had an electric lift for patients in wheel chairs, which was quite a gadget. The temperature of the water was kept at ninety six degrees, just like bath water. It would be nearly impossible to drown in it because it was only four and a half feet deep.

I carefully maneuvered the steps while holding onto the rail. The warmth of the water felt good on my skin. Slowly the warm water was creeping up on my hulk. I liked the heat, but since I was still standing I felt it only a little above my stomach. That wasn't enough. I let my body ease gently into the water, loving every bit. What a wonderful feeling! I wished it would last forever.

My joy was disturbed by one of the patients who began beating the water with her arms, making large splashes. I used to do that when I was a child. I was about to do the same thing, when to my surprise, two other patients went to her side and began hollering, "That's it! Hit it! Hit it hard! Harder! You can hit it harder than that!"

The other patient said, "Doesn't that feel good? Get it all out. You're gonna feel great! Get it all out. It'll feel really good."

In utter amazement I thought, "What are they doing? Should I get out of here?"

I had never seen so much water being splashed by one person. The woman kept splashing for a very long time. The reason for it finally dawned on me. Yesterday's blanket episode had been similar to this when Claudia had tried to free herself from the blanket.

The woman hitting the water finally stopped and let her body flop backwards into the water. She laid there on top of the water, floating like a log. Someone outside of the pool exclaimed, "Very, very good! That was one of the best I have seen. You really made that water splash."

The person who had spoken called out my name, "Ed!"

I acknowledged the call and waded towards her.

Stooping down she said, "I'm Cheryl. I'm your physical therapist. Starting tomorrow, I'll be seeing you three times a week. Today I have the pool duty."

I listened, and thought to myself, every physical therapist I meet is always pretty and seems to have an inborn caring for others.

"Ed, you can try the exercises, or observe what's going on," she said. "But, if you do the exercises, remember this: The moment you feel pain, stop! Don't go any further. Don't overdo it. If it's hurting, stop. Do the exercises up to the point where it is comfortable, with little or no pain. Don't get carried away and create more. You'll discourage yourself from continuing if you push too hard. Do you understand?"

"I think so."

"One more thing. You'll be using muscles that you haven't used before in a long time. This is very important for you. They will hurt for a couple of days. Be prepared for that."

I nodded.

She stood up and cried out, "Everyone to the walls!" The patients waded to their nearest wall and leaned their backs against it. I followed.

"We will start with leg raises. As usual I will demonstrate first."

All the patients except me turned their left sides to the wall, facing the back of the patient in front of them.

Cheryl walked the few steps to the wall behind her. She straightened her body and allowed her left side to barely touch the wall.

"Remember, this is our natural position," she instructed.

It reminded me of standing at attention in the Navy.

"I'm going to raise my right leg slowly upward, in front of me, exhaling at the same time." She did it. She held that position for a moment and said, "Now, I will slowly lower the leg to its natural position inhaling at the same time." She did that and added, "Remember, when you are doing work you exhale. When you return to the natural position, you inhale. You must have that kind of rhythm working to be able to get the full benefit from the exercise." She paused, then cried, "DO IT!"

Not a single person in our group was able to accomplish what Cheryl had done. I tried to lift my leg up and lost my balance. Down under I went, but I easily recovered. The others laughed.

Cheryl continued with her instructions. "Now, I will slowly raise my right leg up and away from the side of my body. Again I will exhale while doing it." She raised her leg out to her side, with the inside of her ankle facing the floor, exhaling as she did so. She paused slightly. "Now, I will lower it to its natural position inhaling at the same time." Her leg returned to its natural position. Again she paused.

"DO IT!" This time her tone seemed sympathetic.

She said, "I have no problem doing this. You do! But, you have the water that creates the buoyancy needed to make it easier. Try any of these exercises outside the pool and you will know what I mean."

I sensed empathy in her instructions and felt very comfortable.

"Lift your leg as far as it will go without hurting. You may not be able to move it at all. You may only be able to lift it a couple of inches. Today, make a mental picture of how far you raised your leg. Do the same with the other exercises. Then you can remember this day, and compare the results with those later on in the program. I'm sure you will be surprised."

I understood what she was saying. I followed her instructions. The exercises showed how immobile and impossible my body was. I was shocked by the simple movements I couldn't do, and yet, I was in the water. It should have been easy. If I were out of the water, I knew I couldn't lift my leg half an inch. Unable to do the exercises, a feeling of awkwardness engulfed me. I became very uncomfortable. I had failed to accomplish any of the exercises. My only success was in trying to do them. Every motion wracked my entire body with pain, but I did try.

"Okay, relaxation time!" Cheryl cried out.

I looked around to see what that meant. The patients were lining up with their backs to the wall of the pool. Arms were stretched out, holding onto the top of the pool. Their bodies rested in the water in different positions.

"Let's all get into a comfortable position." Cheryl waited, then said, "Good!"

I joined the group and found a comfortable position.

"Shake and kick out all those tensions. Send them on their way into the water. Get rid of them."

I expected the water to churn into a turbulent state when the patients started to kick, but barely a ripple formed. Everyone else had pretty much the same disability that I had.

"Okay now!" Cheryl said. "Close your eyes and concentrate on the deep breaths we are going to take." She waited. "Now! Let's take deep breaths. Draw the air in and feel it passing over your lips, drying them, and filling your lungs to capacity. Hold it! Slowly let out all that air. Feel it pass over your lips again. Feel your lips slightly burning from the warm air coming out. Get a mental picture of how all that air entered your lungs, leaving behind the healthy oxygen. See how it gathers all the impurities, and how you are now getting rid of them. Notice that your body should rise slightly from inhaling. This is important. If you do feel a rising sensation, then you're on your way to full relaxation of your body." She paused slightly.

"Exhale! Exhale! Let every bit of that foul air leave you. Don't save any of it. Feel how the oxygen is being absorbed by your body, making it feel better than ever before. Notice how your body is beginning to relax. If your body did rise from inhaling, see if you can feel it fall from exhaling. That rhythm is the key."

Cheryl repeated the exercise three times. A strange, but nice feeling came over me. I had difficulty staying awake. I followed all of her instructions and waited for more. I had never felt such an awareness of water on my skin, or air over my lips. A totally unfamiliar sensation was taking over. I knew then that I was going to like these exercises. Still, I couldn't feel the rise in inhale or the fall in exhale of my body. Maybe it weighed too much.

Cheryl continued, "Now open your eyes lazily and let your legs very slowly feel the cement bottom of the pool. Allow your weight to settle on your legs with that solid feeling of cement under them. Stand up, and slowly stretch your body. Awaken all those muscles that have fallen asleep. Stretch! Stretch! Now you're all awake and ready for the rest of this day."

It was all over. What a beautiful exercise, I thought.

"I don't know why we have to do this silly exercise. I can never see my oxygen going through my body," a patient remarked with exasperation.

"Why can't we just swim?" another patient demanded.

"How can inhaling and exhaling make your body rise? She's gotta be nuts," this patient complained.

I wondered why I liked the exercises when they didn't. We were allowed fifteen minutes of free swimming. I put the minutes into good use. I floated on my back and then on my front. I loved it. I enjoyed every second in that warm water.

It was all over. I showered, dressed, and returned to my room. While preparing for dinner, the relaxed feeling from the pool wouldn't leave me.

Mal came for me, and together we went to the dining room. I asked, "Do you get a good feeling when you're in the pool? It was something great for me! I don't know when I have felt that good in a long, long time."

Mal said, "Sometimes yes, and other times no. Maybe it's my moods."

10

PHYSICAL THERAPY

After breakfast and medical rounds, Mal and I met and left with our group for the P. T. room. I could see stroke patients in their wheelchairs, sitting in whatever position their disabilities allowed them to assume. They made me realize how lucky I was!

As we walked, I talked to Mal about the complaints our pain clinic patients had during medical rounds.

"Everyone complained," I said. "Do any of them have anything else but complaints?"

"Oh, you'll get used to it," Mal said. "Some do have a lot of pain."

"It was depressing. I was glad to get out of there. Will I face that every morning?"

"I don't see how you can avoid it," she answered. "But like I said, you'll get used to it."

We walked into the P. T. room and were greeted by two physical therapists. I had already met Cheryl at the pool. The second therapist was Emma, who went energetically from one person to the other, carrying her clipboard, and getting each person started. Emma was very short, very businesslike, and moved rapidly from one place to another all the time acting like a cheerleader, moving people to try harder. Two bicycles began pedaling to nowhere. A patient sitting in a chair was back bending, as if picking something off the floor.

Emma called out to her in her cheer leading voice, "Roll the top of your head downward, and exhale at the same time. Keep your legs loose. Don't just bend. When you come up, reverse your motions so they will be exactly the opposite of the ones you used on your way down."

The patient paid absolutely no attention to Emma's instructions, just went on at her own plodding and uninspiring pace.

There were two exercising mats that were set about one foot above the floor. A patient began doing leg raises on one. The other was empty except for Cheryl, who was sitting on the edge, writing on her clipboard. I stood waiting for a few moments. Cheryl was definitely pretty. I knew I was going to like being in her company. I decided she would be just right for me to work with. Cheryl was tall, blond and with a comely shape, not too much and not too little.

Cheryl looked up at me, a faint smile on her face, and said, "I see your name here, but I don't know how to pronounce it. Is it okay if I just call you Ed?"

"I understand. It's okay. Not too many people can look at my name and pronounce it right away," I answered rather sheepishly, with a foolish smile on my face.

"You're new here," she, smiling. "Today is a special day for newcomers." She was trying to be comical and continued with, "Ed, sit down next to me, and tell me about your previous P.T. experiences, or if you have ever done physical therapy before."

"Yes," I answered. "I did at some of the other hospitals after my surgery, but it never worked."

She looked very hard at me. No smile this time, just a straight and direct stare.

"Ed, why are you here?"

She asked the question as if I had insulted her. I felt myself turning red, as a sharp burst of pain shot down my leg.

"So I can get rid of my pain!" I quickly said.

"Okay! First rule: You must imbed it in your mind. Physical therapy is what's going to help you get rid of your pain. Follow my instructions. Do them as I ask, and I will guarantee that you will get rid of your pain. Are you willing to work with me to accomplish that?"

"Yes!" I answered guiltily, as though I had done something very wrong. "Definitely! I'll work. I'm here to get rid of my pain. Do you think I want to keep it?"

"Only you can answer that," Cheryl said. "I've heard the same excuses from all the other patients over and over again. All you have to do is look at your group attempting to do the exercises. Are you going to do the same thing they're doing?"

I looked at the others and could see nothing wrong with what they were doing. They were exercising, I thought. Some were on mats on the floor, some were sitting, some were standing, leaning on the walls, and all were performing many different gyrations. I raised my shoulders and nodded slightly.

She noticed what the other patients were doing and said, "They are only going through the motions. Look at their faces. Do they look like they are going anywhere with what they are doing? They are not exercising. They are only going through the motions. Are you going to do the same thing?"

"I'm telling you right now," I answered. "I'm going to do my exercises correctly. I'll do whatever you say. You claim that P. T. will help to get rid of my pain?" I took a deep breath and pulled all the courage together that I could muster and answered, "Well, I am going to prove that you're either right or wrong." I made my statements in dead earnest. Cheryl knew what I meant.

"O.K. I think we understand one another," she said. "I will do the teaching. You do the work."

"Yes! I'm in agreement." We sealed the pact with a handshake. Cheryl gave such a firm handshake that she surprised me. I didn't know what I was letting myself in for, but I felt I had to agree and make a stab at it once and for all. I was as low as I could get, and I had reached the point of no return. What could I lose?

"Let's go to work then."

She stood up, clipboard in hand, and asked me to lie down on the exercise table and do some deep breathing exercises.

I failed the exercise badly. Cheryl asked if I smoked, and I answered, "Yes." She informed me that during the breathing exercise, I was gasping, not breathing.

I didn't know what she meant.

"If you quit smoking, it would help you considerably," she said.

I answered from my lying down position on the mat. I felt awkward and uncomfortable, "I'm trying to quit. I'm trying very hard. I know I'm coughing a lot." I also mentioned my brother who'd died from emphysema, and watching the smoke come out of his throat.

"Did you know that coughing has been proven to create more pain in your back?"

"Yes, I know. Whenever I cough I feel the pain right in my back," I answered, trying to turn and point to the place where the pain was now seizing me, coughing at the same time which made the whole movement fruitless. When the coughing subsided, I answered, "I know I must quit."

"Ed. What a relief to hear you say that! At least now I know you are going to work at stopping smoking, and we here will work with you to have you achieve that goal. You keep on building up your desire to quit. In the meantime, we will teach you how to breathe properly," Cheryl said as she made a mark on the form attached to the clipboard. Then she asked me to lie down on another mat. This mat was about eighteen inches off the floor. It was a little low for me. Anything that low was a real struggle for me, either getting up or sitting down. I eased myself down gingerly. I was beginning to reach the agony stage of my pain. Tension was building and with the tension came more pain.

Cheryl said, "Show me how you get out of bed."

I said, "Whenever I get out of bed, it's torture."

"Show me," she insisted.

I showed her my painful, awkward struggle while she watched. I had to lie down first, then begin to get up.

"No wonder you hurt. If I got out of bed that way my back would hurt too; and I have a healthy back." She marked her paper again.

"Stay seated on the edge of the mat and raise a leg as far as you can without creating any pain."

I tried. I lifted my leg a very little amount and said, "I can't go any further than that. It's hurting."

"You hardly lifted it off the floor!" Cheryl exclaimed.

"You said to only lift as far as I could without creating pain. That was it!"

"I know," she said. She was kind. Compassion showed all over her face. "Have you ever done any exercises, or have you at least walked?"

"No! I was always told to do only bed rest. They told me I was too old for anything else. That's what I did."

"Yes ... I can tell by watching you." Cheryl showed deep compassion, great understanding, as she said, "Don't worry. We'll soon fix all of your problems. We will just have to start from scratch," she said, her voice always so gentle.

"Today, I will show you some exercises to start with. Then you can do the bicycle exercises. But, let me stress this point: Don't overdo. Be careful and deliberate. While you are executing the exercises, do them very slowly, and get a mental picture of what you are doing. Make that a habit."

I asked, "What do you mean by a mental picture?"

"See yourself actually doing the exercise in your mind. Let your mind go through it first. Then, repeat the mental picture as you execute it.

Suddenly, I really felt myself becoming discouraged. My shoulders slumped forward. For all my resolve, it was beginning to fade. It seemed like I couldn't do anything right. It seemed like I couldn't do anything at all.

Cheryl was undaunted by my discouragement that I am sure was beginning to show in my face as well as my body. She just plodded on with a big smile and a brusque command.

"Let's start with your breathing. That's the first thing you must learn before you start any exercises. As you exercise, you exhale as you do the work and inhale when you come to rest."

"I don't understand that." I interrupted. "You mentioned that at the pool. What is work, and what was the other?"

"Do the mental picturing that I just mentioned. Close your eyes. Imagine you're in the pool watching and listening to my instructions. Are you imagining that?"

"I think so," I answered.

"Do you have that picture in your mind, Ed?"

"Yeah, I do."

"Remember me lifting my leg?"

"I got the picture," I said.

"Good!" she said. "I was exhaling while raising that leg. I held it for a second. Then lowered it. That's when I began inhaling, all the way down until the leg came to rest on the floor. The work is the initial part of the exercise. That's when you exhale. When you return to resting position, that's when you inhale."

She gave me an encouraging pat on the arm and urged me by her touch, not to lose faith.

Her words began to make sense to me. I had never been taught how to make mental pictures, or breathe correctly.

I said, "You know, Cheryl, the therapists at the other hospitals never did anything like this. What you said about breathing, that it must coordinate with the work and come to rest, makes sense."

"Looks like we are on our way," Cheryl said with a big smile. She instructed me to lie on my back, place one hand on my abdomen and the other on my chest. I was told to feel my breathing with my abdomen expanding, not my chest. I tried to inhale slowly, through my nostrils, and exhale the same way. I had a lot of trouble.

I was supposed to concentrate on the breath and feel the way it passed through my nose. Then I was supposed to follow it down to my abdomen. Finally, I would exhale and feel it's warmth coming out of my nose. Cheryl knew the difficulty I was having with it all, but her sympathy and understanding were plain to see. I knew she was going to be very important to me. I liked her.

"One more thing," she said. "Get up and walk. I want to see how you walk."

"Walk," I thought to myself. "Am I doing that wrong, too?" I felt like a baby, starting all over again.

Getting up from the exercise table must have been a sight to behold. I could not do it with grace. I could barely do it at all. I struggled and she helped. I had to roll onto my knees first and then hold on to something strong before trying to rise up from such a low position. Eventually I was in an upright position. I started to walk. I didn't go far when Cheryl said, "Just as I thought. You don't know how to walk either," she said with a sigh. "You're dragging a leg. We are not meant to drag our legs. Why are you doing it?"

"It hurts!" I answered. "I'm keeping the pain behind me. I don't want it to come in. It's what everyone else does."

At this point, after the exercises, the discouragement, and the effort to walk, I felt I would cry at any moment.

"Oh, Ed," Cheryl said. "You won't be doing that much longer. You and I have a lot to learn together."

I said, "You didn't expect me to be an easy patient, did you? I didn't want to make it too simple for you. This way I'll get your attention." Being uncomfortable and close to tears, I felt my only recourse was to joke. I had always done that when in a difficult situation.

"You'll have a lot of my attention. You sure will." She smiled.

"First, before anything else, I am going to show you how to get out of bed. If you learn how to do it properly, you won't find it so difficult getting up. I am moving my body to the right side of this table. The left side is the one I will be getting out of. I will bend my right knee, pulling up my foot until it is flat on the bed. It must be as near flat as possible on the bed. Now I will raise my arms and clasp my hands. I am taking a deep breath. As I exhale, I will turn onto my left side in one easy, rolling motion. I will press down on my right foot and make the roll at the same time. Before I deliver the message to my brain, I will visualize the procedure that I am about to do. I will execute it as I visualize it."

I watched and tried to picture in my mind what she was doing. Picturing it was very difficult.

Cheryl continued, "Now I'm on my left side, and I will tuck my left elbow as close to my body as is comfortable. My arm is bent at the elbow. My hand is facing upward, and my right hand clasps the left hand firmly, as if in a handshake. My knees are bent close to the chest. I am visualizing what I am going to do, and I take a deep breath. On the exhale, I again execute what I visualized, all at the same time."

She makes it look so easy.

"I can feel the force coming from my right hand onto my left, pushing my body upward, as my legs roll off the bed in a slow motion. My back is still in a straight position. I allow the weight of my legs to go down to the floor. As you can see I am now sitting on the edge of the bed, and I did not strain any part of my back. When you learn this it will be a pleasure for you to get out of bed."

I watched her very carefully. We changed places. While on the table, I tried what she had shown me, but failed miserably. Visualizing what I was supposed to do was an enormous task for me. The series of moves that Cheryl had gone through were hard to remember. I couldn't recall any of them. She knew it, too. She put me through each move again. I tried to remember them, but time had run out.

Our Physical Therapy sessions only lasted an hour. At the end of the hour, Cheryl gave me some simple leg raises, body twists, and neck exercises to work on. I was to do them as often as I could. I thanked her for working with me and assured her that I would work hard on my exercises. I left with my sponsor, and we headed back to our rooms. I was beyond tears. I was bordering on defeat.

11

ED'S CONSTELLATION

Every Monday, Wednesday, and Friday, at two o'clock, my group meets for a psychomotor session. Today, Wednesday, would be my second experience with this unaccustomed form of psychotherapy. Why was it that when there was something I didn't want to do, the clock ticked faster until it was time to go?

Mal entered my room. "Hey, Ed, it's time for psychomotor! Are you ready?"

I wanted to say no, but fumbled a, "Yes, I'm ready. But, I don't want to go."

"Oh, come on, Ed. It's not going to hurt you. After today, you'll be a pro at it. I also know it will be very good for you."

"Yeah, sure," I muttered.

I took a new pack of cigarettes out of my drawer and walked out of the room with her. My pain, as always, coursing down my left leg.

Out in the hallway, Claudia was fast approaching. Claudia, Mal and I were in the same group, and she was on her way to the session. The image of her torments and struggles under that blanket stuck in my mind. I blinked quickly to get rid of it. I hoped she would ignore us and pass by.

"Hi, Ed!" she said. "Welcome to our Pain Unit." Her voice vibrated with her pleasure, lilting like a bird, and her hand rested companionably on my arm.

My immediate response was to pretend I didn't hear her. Still, the words had been said, and with them, Claudia had been friendly. I couldn't pretend.

"Hi!" I said, and in an undertone offered, "I'm glad to be here."

I wondered what was wrong with Claudia. Everything about her seemed perfectly healthy to me. Even with the burden of a broken marriage facing her, you would never know she was troubled. She acted bubbly, friendly and smiling all the time. We continued towards the psychomotor room. We entered the room. Charley was already inside, waiting. He was talking with Agnes. When I walked in he greeted me politely and continued talking to Agnes. Within seconds, the remainder of my disparate group and the staff assembled in the meeting room. We all sat in a circle.

Charley greeted all of us and before he could finish Claudia interrupted with, "I want a contract."

Charley listened, then asked, "Are you sure, Claudia?"

I looked around at the group and found only stony faces and not a stir from anyone. I wondered what a contract was.

Claudia answered, "Yes, I'm sure."

"What do you want in your contract?" Charley asked.

Claudia seemed a bit nervous and answered, "I want the contract to last two weeks. During the first week, I want to decelerate, and at its end to be free of all drugs. I want to start the second week free of drugs. At the end of the second week, I will go home."

Charley raised his hand to his beard and began stroking it. He didn't seem to embrace the idea. Instead, he gazed around the group and asked, "Does anyone object to Claudia's contract?"

"Yes! Yes!" could be heard from a majority of the group.

"Okay!" Charley said. "Who wants to object first?"

Mal volunteered and said, "Claudia, two weeks is not enough time for your contract. You have been into your limit of medication for a long time. One week of deceleration is no way near enough time. Two weeks would be better. That would allow your body to easily enter a drug-free state. You and I have seen patients decelerating in a week's time, and none of them made it. I'm suggesting a three-week contract. Two weeks of deceleration, and one week of being drug free."

The group simultaneously voiced, "Yeah, that's the only way."

Charley spoke, "What do you think Claudia?"

Claudia could see she was not succeeding with the group. She seemed crushed. "I don't want to stay here anymore. I want to go home. I just want to go home. I know Mal is right. I guess I just wanted to speed it up."

"Do you agree with the decision to wait three weeks? Charley asked.

Claudia replied in a muted tone, "I agree."

"When do you want to start the deceleration?"

"I want to start tomorrow."

"It shall be done."

Charley confirmed the contract and asked Agnes to make a note of it, then said, "I wish you all the luck in the world, Claudia. You've done a good job. Remember, if at anytime you wish to cancel your contract you may. Is that clear?"

She smiled her answer, her eyes beaming into his.

Charley was so pleased. He was always this way when there was a success in sight. He walked over to Claudia and gave her a hug as she rose to greet him.

Charley returned to his seat. He seemed to be able to shift gears quickly as he looked at me and said, "Ed, I know this is new to you. You might as well know what a contract is now that it has been brought up. A contract is about reaching the end of your stay here at the Pain Unit. The patients are heavily medicated in order to be as comfortable as possible to do all the exercises. When the patient feels ready to leave the Pain Unit, he or she calls for a contract to allow enough time to decelerate from the medications. Three weeks is usually plenty. Do you understand, Ed?"

"I guess I do," I answered.

"Let's get on with it then," Charley said. He then looked at me. "At our last meeting, I didn't have a chance to explain what psychomotor was about, Ed."

I looked straight at him, but avoided eye contact.

He said, "Each person must take a thirty-minute turn."

His voice was soft, pleasant, and had a soothing tone. Sometimes it was difficult for me to hear him. I had to strain, but I would never ask him to repeat anything.

"That thirty minutes is your time," he said. "You can use it in anyway you want. You don't have to say anything, but you must take a turn. If you have something private you want to talk about, I'll clear the room. As we become more involved, you will have a better understanding of the structures for releasing anger. Then, if you wish to use them you can. That's about it, Ed. Do you have any questions?"

Automatically, I said, "No!" I didn't know what I could ask.

"If we are all ready, let us begin," Charley waited a moment. Then he said, "Ed, will you start?"

I was jolted by what Charley had said. I was scared. I was so scared I nearly fell out of my chair from a blast of pain exploding at the base of my spine. The fact that he asked me to be next created the tension, causing the pain.

"You really want me to start?"

"Yes," Charley affirmed. "I definitely do want you to be next."

"I don't know where to start," I said.

How could my pain be any worse than it was now? I began breathing very heavily. Perspiration filled my forehead; I could feel my face glistening. No one seemed to notice what I was going through.

I cleared my throat, and wincing with pain, said, "I don't know what to say."

Charley spoke sternly, but his words carried a comforting tone with them. "You're going to have to start sometime. It might as well be now."

I said nothing, and waited. I waited some more. The silence was getting to me. I decided to speak. I couldn't stand the silence any more. I cleared my throat. "What do you want me to talk about?"

"Whatever comes to your mind," Charley answered.

"My mind is blank. Nothing wants to come in. Now what do you want me to do?"

"Keep working at it. Something will come."

I looked around the room and avoided any eye contact. I never liked looking into someone else's eyes. I looked at their stomachs, their shoes, or their hair. I usually found hair interesting. Everyone wears hair differently.

I looked back at Charley and said, "I can't think of anything."

"Like I said Ed, it'll come."

"Take a deep breath," Kay suggested. "Take two or three. That helps. Then say whatever comes to your mind."

I took a deep breath and was taking my second when my mind went back to the sessions at the clinic. I said, "I had no problem talking during the sessions at the clinic."

"What did you talk about at the clinic?" Charley asked.

"I talked about my daughter."

"Go on."

I was embarrassed. Each answer ended with my nervous laugh. I was afraid to reveal my personal problems, afraid to let them know I was unable to handle my daughter. I knew fathers were always supposed to be in control of the situations at home. The thought of revealing my weakness in this area was difficult to bear. I didn't want to tell them. Then, to my surprise, I heard myself plunging right into it.

"You remember those sessions at the clinic back where we live? We went to those sessions at the clinic because of our daughter. My wife and I couldn't handle her."

I glanced around our circle expecting a reaction. There wasn't any.

"She had been taking drugs and smoking pot. She just wouldn't behave. She had been at a halfway house for rehabilitation, but it didn't work. She had gone to another place, and that didn't work either. We just didn't know what to do. A friend of ours suggested the mental health clinic. He said that this clinic had some success with teenagers like my daughter, so we tried it. Now, instead of having our daughter go, my wife and I found ourselves attending sessions. I don't understand what happened. My daughter is the one who needed it. Instead, my wife and I ended up getting the therapy. It's just weird."

"What did you mean by, 'handling her?'" Charley asked.

"You know ... doing the right thing. Trying to teach her right from wrong. You know ..."

"No, I don't know, Ed."

"You know what I mean. I don't want her on drugs or dealing with the wrong kind of people."

"I know that, Ed. What I want to know is what you meant by 'handling' her. Do you mean by 'handling her' actually using your hands?"

He waited for an answer.

"Well, if I had to use my hands, I would. I don't believe in spare the rod and spoil the child. I feel if she deserves a spanking, she deserves it."

"In other words, you would use your hands in handling her. Am I correct in saying that, Ed?"

I tried to understand what he meant. There was a feeling growing inside of me that told me something I was doing was wrong. My pain continued to make me feel uncomfortable. It was forcing me to change my position in my seat. The more I moved, the more pain I would create. I wondered whose side this guy was on. I was growing angry.

I answered, "Yes, I would use my hands." I thought I'd said it with conviction. I searched the faces of the others, waiting to be reinforced. The reinforcement didn't come. I was beginning to dislike this interaction. I wanted no more of it. I felt as if I was the person who was wrong.

"Look," I said, "I feel as if you're all trying to make me feel guilty about something."

"No, Ed. I'm not trying to do that at all."

I knew my discomfort was showing. Charley changed the subject, probably to distract me.

"I want to hear something about Ed," Charley prompted. "Tell me about your mother and father, and that part of your family."

"My parents were both born in Poland. I think they met on their way over here. Something during their ordeal with the Russians made them decide to emigrate to the U.S. I don't know if their meeting was in Poland, or aboard the ship, or when they got here. They married and settled. They had eight children, six boys and two girls."

I added, with pride, that my parents had received an award from our President and the Cardinal for providing six sons to the war effort. My parents proudly displayed their six stars on a small flag in our front room window, for everyone who passed by to see.

"What was your family constellation?" Charley asked.

I paused, then answered, "What does that mean?"

"In what position were you born? First, second, third, or last?"

"Oh! There were five brothers first. Then came my older sister, me, and then my younger sister." I saw Charley`s red beard move. Something I had said seemed to get to him. He spoke so softly that I didn't hear. My mind was focussed on stopping this conversation. I wanted to quit. I said, "I can't go on anymore. I have to stop."

Charley agreed. "That was good, Ed. It was very interesting. We do have something to go on now. We will pursue it further next time."

Next time! I hoped there would be no next time. I didn't like this session at all. I was completely drained and in a considerable state of confusion.

12

AGNES ... STOP

The days at the Pain Unit went by in a drug-induced haze. The routine was the same but varied with its problems. We all went from one activity to another with different attitudes, some willing, some not, others complaining. And I, I was just plain nervous and unwilling to expose my feelings and my past. I was anxious, confused and in pain from one end of the day to the other. I smoked constantly. I was scared and feeling hopeless but at the same time I wanted to make a success of this experience. I was determined to leave pain free, whereas the others seemed to have no desire at all except to spend time here, get by the best they could, then leave.

Today, we were in the psychomotor session when Charley announced in front of everyone, "Ed, we have some unfinished business from the last session. I'm going to start with you."

I was startled. Why me? Why do I have to be first? I was about to say I'm not ready, when Charley spoke.

Charley said, "Last time, Ed, we spoke of your constellation. You now know what that means. Is that correct?"

Nodding, I said, "Yes."

Charley continued, "You said that there were eight children in your family. Five boys came first, then a sister, then you, and then another sister. Am I correct?"

Again I nodded. I wondered why he was mentioning that. There were eight kids in our family. So what?

"Did you get along with your brothers?" Charley asked.

"I hardly ever saw them," I answered. "They were much older than I, and all worked."

"Can you remember anything specific about them?" Charley asked.

I thought for a moment. "Yes, one of my brothers was very sick. I was about four or five years old. I can remember a crowd of people in our front room where he was lying in a bed. There were candles lit all over. The people seemed to be moaning something. I think he was receiving the last rites of the church. Everyone was attending to him."

"Did he get a lot of attention when he was sick?" Charley asked.

"Yes, for two or three days, he was getting all kinds of attention."

"Anything else, Ed?"

"I remember my two older brothers always fought."

"You mean they hit each other?"

"No, no, they argued very loud. I can remember one day, I was told to go outdoors, and as I walked outdoors by the living room, I could hear them hollering. They were so loud. My father was screaming at them. Whenever they fought I was sent out of the house. Boy, was I scared! I ran out of my yard."

"Anything else?"

"One time I was very disappointed. My second oldest brother was a paratrooper who fought in North Africa. He wrote me a letter. I was very surprised to get a letter addressed to me. No one ever wrote to me. It was the first letter I'd ever received. He said he'd captured a motorcycle, it belonged to a German and he took it. Then he rode all around with it. He also cut hair in his battalion, like a barber, and made extra money doing it. At the end of the letter, he said that if there was anything I wanted, I was to write to him, and he would send it to me. I was so excited, I sat right down and wrote a letter to him. I asked him for a baseball glove, the only thing I ever wanted. Then the youngest of the five …

"Wait a minute!" Charley demanded. "Did you get the glove?"

"No, no. I never got it," I said.

"You never got it?"

"Nope," I whispered.

"Was there anything else?"

"I started to say that the youngest of the five brothers took me swimming. He was always good to me, and always stuck by me when my sister accused me of something. I knew he was a good swimmer and wanted him to teach me. I already knew how to dog-paddle. He took me to the canal where everyone swam naked. Usually, I watched the others swim and wished I could. I would slip into the water a few feet from the bridge close to the wall and dog-paddle to the bridge where I could grab onto the pipes underneath it, or hold onto the wall. It was fun, but I wanted to swim like the others, from one bridge to the other in the center of the canal. On this particular day I went with him. I was standing on the bridge, naked like the others, and my brother pushed me into the canal. I was frightened out of my wits. I could hear him say, 'Swim, Ed! Swim!' I thought I would drown. I was so scared. I did my dog-paddle furiously and was able to get to the wall and hold on. My brother came over and pulled me out. I was gasping for breath and near tears, but I didn't cry. Then he began showing me how to do the overhand stroke. That's how I learned to swim."

"Were you able to swim after that?" Charley asked.

"Oh, yes. I learned how to swim and was able to race like the others from bridge to bridge."

I stopped for a moment, reflecting on the past, and then said, "That's about it."

"That's good, Ed. How about your sisters? Did you get along with them."

I groaned and said, "My oldest sister always got me in trouble. Whatever she did wrong, she always blamed me. My mother would punish me, or tell me, 'Wait till your father gets home. He'll take care of you.' I never wanted my father to come home. My sister would pass by me, punch me, and run, screaming 'Eddie hit me! Eddie hit me!' I got blamed but I never did touch her. I used to get so angry at her.

"Once I went to the bathroom. She placed the top of a chair under the doorknob so I couldn't open the door. My mother had gone shopping. I tried the door and it wouldn't open. I thought it was stuck. Then I realized it was forced shut. I screamed and screamed for her to open it. Finally, I climbed out the window. Was she surprised to see me! I told my mother when she came home. My sister denied every bit of it, but my mother didn't punish her, she punished me. Was I ever angry!"

"How about your younger sister, Ed? Did you get along with her?" Charley asked.

"Yeah, she was all right. We got along and played together. She was closer to my age. Maybe that's why."

I kept silent for a minute. Again I felt embarrassed and foolish, as though I had said too much. "That's it. I can't think of anything else."

"That's all very interesting," Charley said. He stroked his beard again. I could only see his eyes and beard. He seemed to do that every time he became thoughtful, reflecting on some point of interest.

"You mentioned that you were very angry. Were you angry while recalling that episode, Ed?"

"I don't know. I did feel something. It may have been anger."

I could see that Charley's eyes were closed and wondered what he was thinking. There was a very long pause. I was getting nervous. Charley finally spoke.

"Ed, I want to do a structure with you."

"I don't want to get under a blanket!" I nearly screamed it at him.

"You do have a lot of anger inside you, Ed. Sooner or later, you're going to have to release it. It can only help you. But that isn't what I want you to do now. I want you to choose either Agnes or Kay for this structure. Whichever one you choose will stand over there at the door. At my signal, she will walk toward you. When you want her to stop, raise your right or left hand. Do you understand?"

I understood. But what's that all about? I thought. Why does he want her to do that?

"Ed! Do you understand?" Charley asked again.

"I'm sorry. Yes, I do," I said, my voice very timid at this point in time. "How close do you want her to be before I raise a hand?"

"That's up to you. Raise it when she gets close enough for you to become uncomfortable and want her to stop."

"Must I do this?" I asked.

"No, you don't have to, I won't force you to," Charley answered, "although it would be to your advantage. This structure would give me more information to use for dealing with your pain. We know that your pain isn't only coming from your back. It's coming from somewhere else. We must find ways to prove that to you. It's a matter of sharpening your awareness to everything around you."

I knew he was talking about something that was beyond my understanding. I felt hopeless once again but decided to go along with him.

"Agnes. I want Agnes to do it," I said reluctantly.

"Good, Ed."

"Agnes, will you accommodate Ed in this structure?"

Agnes smiled in agreement, and spoke at the same time, "Yes, of course I will."

Agnes was always so agreeable, I wished she had said no. Would have made it all much easier for me.

"Good!" Charley said. "Let me know when you're ready, Agnes."

I could feel the tension building in the room. It built up not only for me, but for the rest of the group. The other members of the group did not stir an inch. No one moved. I saw a nod of assent coming from Agnes to Charley.

Charley spoke, "Shall we get on with it?"

Agnes got up and walked toward the door, stopped in front of it, and turned to face me.

My chair was positioned in a direct line toward her. She was about fifteen feet away.

Charley spoke again, this time with extreme caution and in a kindly tone of voice, "Ed, if you want Agnes to stop, just raise your right or left hand. She will immediately comply. Is that understood?"

Along with my nervous laughter, and clearing of throat, I said, "Yes. I understand."

"Agnes, you will walk toward Ed? If at any time Ed raises a hand, you are to stop. If I say stop, you are also to stop. Do you understand, Agnes?"

"Yes, I do," she answered. "Not only do I stop when Ed raises a hand, I also stop when you tell me."

"That's correct," Charley said.

Again there was a pause, but this time it filled the room with an air of curiosity. Charley used this pause to study the scene he had just created. He finally broke the silence.

"Agnes! Start walking towards Ed."

Agnes nodded and began to take slow deliberate steps toward me. My eyes automatically focused on her breast. I knew my face was flushed. I hoped she didn't notice and wondered if all men did that. Quickly, I moved to other parts of her body. I began scanning her skirt, arms, and then back to her breast. With each scan, more blood flowed to my face, making it more flushed. I hoped that she didn't notice my eyes constantly scanning her breasts.

I looked straight at her, and at the same time, searched, for a comfortable sitting position. The effects of my back operations were turning me into a target at a firing range. The red-hot bullets were piercing my back and ricocheting down both legs creating the worst of pain. I kept searching for a comfortable position as she walked, deliberately, and slowly. It seemed as if each step she was taking was one of the bullets shooting into my back. My body was stiffening.

Agnes was getting closer. I could feel beads of sweat appearing on my upper lip, my forehead, and the sides of my face. The beads swelled to droplets. They began flowing downward, collecting at my shirt collar, and drenching it. My breathing became heavier. My body became stiffer. The pain was becoming unbearable. I had to stop her.

I raised my hand. It didn't go up! I looked at it. Get up there! No one heard me, not even my hand. I'd lost my voice!

I looked at my left hand, GO UP! It didn't hear me. Agnes was about five feet away from me. I felt as if I was going to be bowled over and flattened by a steamroller. Nothing would move. Even my lips refused to cry out. Panic began to overtake me. My eyes were glued to this body moving towards me. They wouldn't move towards Charley, to plead with him to stop her. This was frightening! Why was it happening? Scream! That's it! I'll scream!

"Stop! Stop Agnes!"

It wasn't my voice! It was Charley's. I couldn't say it. I couldn't stop her.

Relief! It had ended. It was over, but why couldn't I stop her?

I was breathing heavily and drained completely from the ordeal. The group was motionless. I stared at Charley. I wanted some answers, but I didn't know what questions to ask. If Charley was conveying any message, his beard masked it. I couldn't read anything coming from him.

Charley finally spoke, "I'm aware of how agonizing and painful that ordeal was for you Ed. A complete analysis of what is really going on cannot be fully explained at this time. I need to sort it out. There is no question about you being dominated by women." He paused a moment, explored my face with his eyes then carried on with what he was saying. "Consider your constellation. You were born into a large family with five male siblings first, then a female sibling, then you, and finally another female sibling. That's a complicated and interesting constellation. It demands more information from you, for me to properly sort and to know where you're coming from."

He also explained, "Love and attention are needed for normal growth. I feel certain you didn't get either of them. Then, the question arises, how did you deal with that? But, we must stop now. Time has run out. We will continue this next time."

I wasn't sure about wanting a next time. I got up slowly from my chair and walked out with the others. I had so many questions to ask. I wanted answers. I wanted to know why that happened to me. No one else in the room existed at that moment. I looked at no one and went immediately to my room.

13

SENSORY AWARENESS

Susan hugged me. I'd never seen her before. Mal and I had just walked into the room for our sensory awareness session. She came over and hugged me, just like that. I didn't know what to do. My face flushed, and my body stiffened. I was embarrassed.

"Welcome to sensory awareness, Ed," she said while hugging me. She let go, stepped back, and said, "My name is Susan." She read my body language. "Has anyone ever hugged you, Ed?"

I blurted, "No! Only my wife."

"Were you ever been hugged as a child?" Susan asked.

"You mean hugged when I was growing up?"

"Yes," she answered.

"I ...don't think so. I can't remember."

"Do you hug your children?" Susan asked.

"No. My wife does that. I don't have to do it." I was getting annoyed.

"Ed, hug me," her voice was encouraging.

Again, I flushed. What was she trying to do to me? "I can't do that. You're not my wife," I said.

"Please, Ed, hug me." Her eyes penetrated into mine.

Those eyes hypnotized me into hugging her. It felt good, but what would my wife think? I held the hug for a second, then backed away.

"Thanks, Ed. It felt good."

I knew she lied. There was hardly any squeeze in her hug.

Susan backed away, turned, greeted other patients, and hugged some. She started the session with a breathing exercise.

Susan must have noticed my dilemma. My body language gave it away when my face reddened and my body stiffened. I really liked what she did, but didn't know how to react. I'd never been hugged by anyone except Mary. It never entered my mind to be hugged by someone else. I guess it was okay, but not with men.

Susan was like gravity. People were drawn towards her. Every part of my body reacted to her. I liked it. Is this what falling in love was all about? Just looking at her was an experience. It was also strange not to feel any sexuality toward her. She exuded comfort and warmth, and I wanted to be near her. It couldn't be love. Mary was my only love.

We started the breathing exercise by sitting erect with our feet flat on the floor. Susan always used the same words: "Take in a deep breath. Feel it coming in. Hold it. Let it out slowly, and feel it going out." I guessed anything we did here began with a deep breath. I could almost predict it. Whether I liked it or not, I was going to learn how to breathe.

While we were breathing, Susan began explaining the purpose of the exercises. They had something to do with getting our minds in touch with our bodies and sharpening our awareness.

Next, Susan had us all stand up and close our eyes. She asked us to start walking and to notice what was happening. It was strange. Now I knew how a blind person felt. It was difficult to keep my eyes closed. I kept bumping into others. At each contact I would open my eyes, even though I wasn't supposed to. Susan kept repeating, "Keep your eyes closed! Keep your eyes closed!" It was nearly impossible to do.

"Okay! That's enough. Take your seat," Susan said. She added, "Your eyes have experienced light and darkness. The more you are aware, the more you know."

I wondered why she placed so much emphasis on awareness. That word was constantly used.

Susan continued, "Now, I will demonstrate the art of massaging legs. Each of you will be given a partner with whom to demonstrate what you have learned."

I turned red as a beet, hoping no one noticed. I'm sure my body shook at the thought of massaging someone else's legs. I had never even massaged my wife, let alone anyone else. What if my partner were a girl? What would I do then? What if I got an erection? The questions haunted me. I knew I couldn't massage anyone. What were they trying to do here? The whole session was disturbing to me. Maybe I could get sick and have to leave. Maybe this was just a dream.

Susan said, "Our blood flows in one direction. It goes from the heart, to the front of the head, down the back, up the front, returning to the heart, and starts the cycle all over again. That's the direction we will take with the leg massage."

I knew she had to pick someone to demonstrate what she had explained. I hoped it wouldn't be me, but I was chosen. Susan asked me to raise my pant legs above the knees. The group began whistling and cat calling. I enjoyed the attention and mimicked a stripper. They all laughed.

Susan sat on the floor in front of me, with a jar and a towel. She had some special coconut cream jelly in the jar. First, she rubbed minute quantities of it into the palm of her hands. Then she told us that our body temperature would liquefy the cream, and to warm it so that our legs wouldn't feel a sudden shock of cold when it was applied. Her thumbs began rubbing along the front of my leg, up towards the knee. At the knee, her fingers rubbed down the back of my leg to the ankle. As she came down, her thumbs were not touching the front of my leg.

While doing the massage she said, "I'm helping to move the blood up toward the knee and helping it to come down toward the ankle. I'm following the flow of the blood. I'll repeat it several times." She did. "Now, I'll switch to the other leg and repeat the massage the same amount of times, to keep them balanced."

There was no question about the effects of the massage on my legs. I was mesmerized. It felt so good, but the fear about what would happen to me when I did the massage to someone else was getting stronger. Susan finished and wiped down my legs with a towel, removing the oily cream. She asked me to get up very slowly, to make certain my feet were on the floor, and to take a careful step. I obeyed and remarked, "What a wonderful feeling!"

"Now, it's your turn," Susan said. "I want you to choose a partner, but chose someone from the opposite sex," she said.

Why do my fears always come true? I thought. No matter what it was, whatever I feared became real. I had to choose a female. I looked at all the women and chose one who looked older than I did. Maybe I would feel safer with someone older. I went over to my choice and asked her if she would be my partner. She accepted.

Susan began instructing us on the art of leg massaging, following the same procedure she did to mine. I was going to have two massages.

My partner's massage lacked the firm control Susan had applied. I could almost feel the blood being hastened upward when Susan rubbed. That feeling was not there with my partner. She barely touched my skin, but it still felt good. I knew, after experiencing a good massage, I would try to give one to my partner.

"Make sure you even up the strokes on each leg," Susan said. "Let's finish it off. When you're all done, wipe the legs with the towels to remove the oil."

Susan waited, and when we were all done she said, "Reverse positions, and let the men do the work this time."

I massaged my partner's legs and enjoyed every minute of it. She, too, enjoyed it. While I massaged, none of my previous fearful thoughts entered my mind. I knew my rubbing was firm and deliberate, and I concentrated on the blood flow. I seemed to even imagine the blood being pushed. I had no doubts that my partner was enjoying it.

"Okay, even it off and wipe it dry," Susan said.

I did that. My partner was surprised at how effective my massaging was. She said her legs would never be the same. She might call on me again. I was a little embarrassed because everyone heard her.

I thought of trying it on Mary. What a surprise that would be for her! She had never had a leg massage. The next time she visited me she would get one.

Strangely, this session produced no shots or stabbing of pain like the others had. The sensations were bearable, and I didn't have to think about them. Why? I thought.

14

AN OBJECT

Two weeks had passed. I wondered if everyone experienced such weird and bizarre events during their life. Was it just me? Memories of how anger was dealt with in the book I had read, *The Primal Scream*, flashed through my mind. I had never dreamed of living through similar experiences. I wondered what the following week had to offer.

I reflected on the past week and was surprised at what I had accomplished: walking three laps, losing three pounds in three days, and doing seven exercises three times twice a day. The massages every day were pure ecstasy. The pool, with its 96-degree temperature, should be in every home. The other activities, psychomotor, sensitivity awareness, and rap sessions, were still alien to me and difficult to grasp. Strangely though, I was looking forward to them again.

Some patients were able to go home for the weekend if permitted by their insurance companies. The Pain Unit had a standing rule that patients had to stay for the first two weeks before they could go home.

Mary and our two girls came to visit. I expected our son, Eric, to come with them but for some reason he chose to stay with his grandmother that day. I excitedly began to tell them about my first week. I offered to massage Mary's legs, but she refused. She was angry. She was still too angry because I was in the hospital. I was disappointed, but Susan said, "Do me, Dad, do me." I did. She loved it; Amy wanted it, too. A strange and unusual closeness toward my girls overcame me as I massaged their legs. Their joy from the massage had entered my hands, creating an affection for them I'd never had. My body absorbed every bit of that feeling. Then they both hugged me tighter than ever. I knew then what sensory awareness was all about. A huge change was taking place within me. I knew it.

I got up the next morning to start a new week and went through what had turned out to be my daily routine of having an ice massage, fetching my medicine, showering, doing laps, then eating breakfast. After the doctor's rounds, I went on to the scheduled activities.

I was preparing to get ready for a rap session when a voice echoed.

"Ed! You treat me like an object."

I turned quickly to see who had said it. Two aides had just entered the room. I couldn't tell which one had said it.

Dumbfounded, I asked, "What do you mean?"

Betsy said, "You treat me like an object."

My eyes failed to see any other object in the room to which she could be referring.

The other aide, Marty, whom I really disliked, agreed with her, "She's right, Ed. You treat us like objects." She crossed her arms and stood there looking at me with a piercing stare.

I raised my arms helplessly, hands extended, and said, "I don't know what you mean." I stared at them, wondering what this was all about.

I asked, "What does that mean, treating you like an object? We are all some kind of an object. How should I treat you any differently than anything else?"

They obviously didn't understand my confusion. One of them said, "Well, you treat us like that chair—an object. You ..."

I interrupted; I was growing irritated. I didn't know what was happening. "But I have respect for that chair. It's on loan to me in this room, and I'll take good care of it. So, what's wrong with that?"

Marty stated in a flat, gruff voice, "We are not chairs, Ed!"

"I know you're not a chair, but I do respect you. I don't understand what you're saying. We're all some kind of an object."

"That's the point, Ed. We're not like a chair. We're not objects. We're human beings who have feelings, very strong feelings. The two of us, as humans, sense that you are treating us like objects. We think ..."

I interrupted again, "How am I supposed to treat you then?"

Betsy asked sweetly, "Can we play a little game with you?"

"Yeah, okay," I mumbled.

She continued, "I'll stay here, sitting on this chair, reading. I want you to notice what happens when my partner walks out of the room and returns again."

"Okay!" I agreed. "What do you want me to do?"

"Do whatever you want, but make sure you notice everything that goes on."

Marty left the room, and the other sat in the chair pretending to read a magazine. I went over to the window and peered out.

Marty walked back in and said, "Hi Betsy!"

I turned and looked at her. She walked towards Betsy, keeping her eyes on her, avoiding eye contact with anything else in the room.

"A few of us are going for a walk in about half an hour. Do you want to come along with us?"

Betsy answered, "I would love to! It's a fine day for a walk!"

Marty bent over and began to whisper something into Betsy's ear. I couldn't hear what was said, but I heard them both laugh. They kept whispering and laughing. Finally I heard, "I must go now. We'll meet in a half hour at the nurse's desk, okay?" She walked out of the room.

A few moments later, Marty came back into the room and asked, "Ed, how do you feel about what just happened?"

"I feel all right," I answered.

"What happened when I walked into the room and went straight to Betsy?"

"Nothing that I could see."

She asked, "Didn't you feel slighted when I didn't say hello to you while I was walking into the room?"

"No! Not at all!"

"Didn't you feel as if you were left out? Didn't all my actions give you the impression that you weren't in the room? We ignored you completely. Didn't it bother you?"

"It didn't bother me," I said, reluctantly. "What am I supposed to do? Hug you every time I see you and say you're not a chair or an object?"

"No, Ed. That's not what I mean."

I knew they were trying to tell me something that was meant to be some kind of help to me, but I couldn't figure it out. The more they tried to explain it the more confused I got. I put my arms around Betsy and asked, "Is this what you mean?"

They both laughed, "No, Ed. That's not what we mean."

I could feel tears welling up in my eyes. I wanted to understand what they were trying to tell me but it just wouldn't happen.

"That's all right," Betsy said.

I could feel compassion coming from Betsy. That made me want to weep. Marty showed only annoyance and frustration. At that point, they indicated it was time to leave.

I stood there totally confused. I didn't feel very good about myself for some reason, but I didn't know what the reason was.

"It's okay, Ed. We're just trying to make a point. It's probably too soon for you to understand. But in time, you will. When it happens it will open a new world for you."

Again, with much frustration, I said, "Tell me what you mean when you say I was treating you like an object"

"Don't worry. You'll find out in time."

Betsy and Marty left. I walked to my bed and fell onto it. I could feel every muscle in my body tightening. My pain was growing worse. I didn't care about objects! All I wanted was more percodans!

15

THE CIRCLE

I sat there in the partly filled circle, waiting for Charley and the others to start the session. I began thinking of him. There wasn't a single drop of negativity in that man. He was so positive about everything. His attitude was reflected in his clothes, his tone of voice, and his beard. He made me feel very comfortable being in his presence. His clothes were simple. He wore earthy-colored corduroy sport jackets, with shirts and ties to match, and dungarees. When he spoke, he never used "you should, you could, you must". His words always carried a sense of understanding of what I was saying when I spoke with him. His body language reinforced all these attributes. I could almost feel myself wanting to discuss with him everything and anything about myself. If there was anyone who could help me, Charley was that person. All I needed was a little more assurance and encouragement.

Charley entered the room, and his usual warm greeting was acknowledged and returned. He ambled over to the empty chair between Agnes and Kay, eyeing everyone on his way, and settled his small frame into it.

His beard always intrigued me. It seemed to glow or glisten whenever he spoke, as if a light were turned on behind it. It wasn't the same color or texture as the hair on his head.

The other patients entered, selected their seats, and when all were settled, formed a crude circle except for one empty chair.

Charley, comfortably seated in his chair, said, "I guess we'll have to wait for Ethal again."

Alex remarked, "Why do we always have to wait for Ethal? Why can't we start without her?"

I agreed with him and said, "She knows we're supposed to be here at one o'clock. I deliberately passed her room on the way over here and saw her lying on her bed reading."

Charley suggested, "Why don't one of you tell her how you feel about her lateness."

"Okay, I will," Alex said emphatically.

Just then Ethal entered and filled the empty seat.

Alex burst out with, "Why are you always late? Can't you be here on time like the rest of us? You don't have to worry about traffic or anything like that. There's no reason for you to be late and keep us waiting!" His tone demanded an answer.

She turned and looked at him, "It's none of your fucking business!"

My chair exploded under me. She was direct and meant every word of it. Alex was agog, too.

Charley remained unmoved. Looking at Alex and me, he said, "At the next session, both of you come in late."

I looked at Alex and said, "I can't do that. Can you?"

Alex answered, "I'm willing to try, to see how it feels."

"How about you, Ed?" Charley asked.

"I guess I can try."

Ethal just sat back in her chair with a smirk on her face.

"Let's start now," Charley said. "Ed, we still have unfinished business here. I'd like you to be first."

I sensed a sigh of relief from the others. I could see their bodies relax from the tension they had held up to that moment. I wanted to pretend not to hear him, and quickly reflected on what I felt about him. A real genuine comfort came over me. He wanted to help me. I decided not to worry about it anymore and do as he asked.

"Okay, Charley. I'll go first."

"Good, Ed," Charley replied. "I want to hear more about you. Let's start with your back. When did you first experience your back pain?"

The tone of his question was comforting and encouraged me to answer. I still had to lower my head, not daring to look at the others, as I fought my fears about talking to a group. My voice cracked, and phlegm gathered in my throat when I tried to speak. Clearing my throat, I began.

"I was working at my brothers' gas station." Again, I had to clear my throat and shifted position in my chair. "One day, I felt a pang in my back. It persisted for a few days, and I couldn't work anymore. One of our customers was a doctor. I asked him about it. He drove me to his office, checked me out, and called it neuritis. He gave me some pills and said to get some bed rest for a couple of days."

"Did it go away?" Charley asked.

"Yes."

"Did you like working at a gas station?"

"No! I hated it!" I said with scorn.

"How long did you work there?"

"A couple of years." I shied away from answering Charley's question accurately.

"A couple of years?" Charley questioned. "I don't understand. Why did you work there if you didn't like it."

I paused and again changed position in the chair, replying meekly, "I had no choice."

"You had no choice? Who was forcing you to work there?"

Again, I answered meekly, feeling much like a small child, "Well ... it was my family. I had to help my brothers."

I thought this was naturally done in families. I wondered why Charley made me feel that I had to convince him of something? I continued. "After my discharge from the Navy, I worked for them at a gas station they leased from an oil company. Soon after, they decided to buy their own gas station in another location. My father insisted I help them, so I loaned my brothers all the money I had saved while in the Navy. With their money and all I had saved, they had enough to make a down payment. I wasn't made a partner but they promised to pay me back. I did what my father asked."

Charley interrupted, "Did they pay you back?"

My eyes fell to the floor. "Yes, eventually, but not with money. They paid me back with gas for my car."

"With gas for your car?" Charley repeated, incredulity ringing in his voice. "Didn't they pay you a salary for working there?"

"I was supposed to get a weekly salary, but most of the time they couldn't pay me. Instead, I would get some spending money whenever I needed it."

"Did that equal a weekly pay?" Charley asked.

"No, it didn't. Wait a minute, I just remembered something!" I changed the subject. It was too painful for me to continue with it any longer. Instead I said, "I was hit in my back by an automobile at a very early age. No one in my family can recall it today. I ran across the street to meet my oldest brother, who had just come out of church. A car struck me. I was in a ward for children at a hospital. Every day, someone came around to entertain us with a hand puppet. I can vividly recall laughing and enjoying the puppet. Everyone there was very nice to me. That hospital left me with fond memories."

"Did anyone come to visit?" Charley asked.

I thought for a moment, "I can't remember. I don't think anyone did."

"Were you hospitalized at any other time?"

"Oh, yes! I sure was!" No longer was I uncomfortable. The words just seemed to flow easily, and my recall was great. Charley's beard seemed to glow a pretty orange-red as I spoke.

"Oh, yes. I had my tonsils out. That was only an overnight. Again, everyone was nice to me. Then I had a deviated septum. That was a scary one. I was in a room that seemed to have an endless amount of beds. The beds and the people in them were everywhere. It was like a nightmare, and I was glad to get out."

"Did your mother or father come to visit you?"

I paused for a moment and said, "I can't remember. As a matter of fact, I don't remember anyone from my family ever coming to visit me."

"No one?" Charley questioned.

"I don't remember anyone."

"Were there any other operations?"

I was warming up to my subject now. I always enjoyed talking about my trips to the hospital. People listened to me. "Yes, when I joined the Navy. I was assigned to a chicken shit cruiser. It was a new ship, but very chicken shit."

"What do you mean by, 'chicken shit'?" Charley asked.

"You were treated like dirt. Nothing was ever done right. It was always hurry up and wait. Tolerance was unheard of.

"One day we had a battle stations exercise. Mine was a second loader. We had to run to our battle stations. Being a second loader was new to me. I followed my group all the way down to the bottom of the ship. I didn't mind that, until I got into this circular room. The hatchway was big enough to let one person go through at a time. I got in and saw a conveyer belt coming out of the floor, and another going out of our room through the ceiling. Our job was to pass the ammo from one belt to the other.

"There were four of us in that room. Then the door closed with a bang! I panicked when the door was latched from the outside. We were locked in. There was no way out of this room. I smelled a rat. This was not for me. Then I asked myself what we would do if we got hit. What would happen? How would we get out? There was no way out!

"This duty was not for me. I had to find a way to get off this ship. A transfer would do it. As quickly as that thought came to me, it was blown apart with another. Seamen second class didn't get transfers. I felt trapped.

"A few days passed when a slight pain in the right side of my groin prompted me to go to Sick Call. The pharmacist said to drop my pants and shorts. I did.

"Aboard ship there was no privacy. Everything was done in the open. Whenever anyone dropped their pants, it was always a sure sign of V.D. Those passing by spared me no mercy. The cat calling was at it's best, drawing many laughs. I enjoyed being the victim. Getting the attention was what I liked.

"The pharmacist looked at the right side of my groin and found a lump. He called the doctor. The doctor examined me. He made me go through the coughing routine and decided to send me to a hospital. With great relief I packed all my gear and went to a Naval Hospital."

"You got off the ship," Charley remarked.

"Yes, I did, and it was Thanksgiving time. The hospital was on holiday routine, and I was able to go home for a five-day weekend leave. I didn't have to report back until Monday morning. I didn't expect that. I was delighted."

"Where did you go on your leave, Ed?"

"I went home. On my return, the doctors thoroughly checked my groin and decided I had a hernia. By this time, the hospital was on Christmas routine, even though it was only the fifth of December. They sent me home again. Only emergencies would be scheduled. They told me to come back on the fourth of January. I would have my operation on the sixth of January. The sixth was the day my ship was scheduled for its six-week shake-down cruise. I would miss it, and get a new assignment. That was luck. I wouldn't have to go back into the battle stations area again. What a relief!"

"Did you have the operation?" Charley asked.

"Yes, I did. And you know, by mistake, they almost operated on the left side not the right. I was all drugged and had to tell them that it was the right side. Someone picked up my chart and agreed with me. Then they switched over to the right side.

"After the surgery and recovery, I was assigned to a refrigeration ship. That was good duty."

"You were very well rewarded." Charley nodded, looking at me very thoughtfully. "Were there any more operations?"

"Yes, there were. During my first semester at college, I had just eaten breakfast and got up to go to class, when a sharp pain struck the side of my left knee. I couldn't walk. My brother took me to the hospital where surgery was required to remove a bone-spur from the inside of my left knee. I went to school with crutches."

"How were you doing in school?" Charley asked.

"The surgery and its recovery left a big void in my studies. I couldn't catch up."

"I mean, how were you doing with your studies before the surgery?"

"Not good, my study habits were poor. I didn't really want to go to school."

"Then why did you go?"

"I don't know. I guess the pressure from my parents, the fact I could go to college under the GI bill, and get paid for going, was a good enough reason."

"Did you like college?"

"Not really. I had trouble understanding what I was to learn. Nothing was making any sense to me. There were too many words whose meanings I didn't understand in the subject areas I was studying. I got tired of looking up the meanings of words. Those I did look up didn't help me to understand."

"Did you pass all your courses?"

"I flunked three. I couldn't catch up because of the operation."

"I see," Charley said as he stroked his beard.

I didn't like the sound of what he said. It bothered me when he said, " 'I see' ". It meant something, something I didn't understand.

"Anymore?"

"Yes! The next semester, an attack of appendicitis required immediate surgery. While I was there, it was suggested that one of my hammer toes should be straightened before serious problems developed. That was taken care of, too."

"How about school?"

"How about school! There was no way I could catch up with my studies. I quit."

"Did you pursue it later?"

"No! I went to work. But I did try night school."

"How did you do then?"

Something was happening to me as I was being questioned. I had a strange feeling that there was a connection between my surgeries and personal tight spots. More questions began developing. Where were the answers? Tension, back pain, they were all coming together now as I sat spewing off about my operations.

"That's ... when ... my back operations began." I said it with a slow deliberate voice.

"Ed, let's hold off on the back operations. Instead, I'd like to do an experiment with you. Would you mind? It could prove helpful."

I was dazed. I said, "No, I don't mind."

He asked Agnes and Kay to get a dozen books or magazines. They obliged. He asked me to move my chair out of the circle and place it in the center. I did and stood away from it. He asked the rest of the group to form a larger circle around my chair. Not a sound came from the group.

They obliged. Agnes and Kay came in with the books and magazines. I watched Charley take the books and make a circle around my chair. Questions built up inside of me while the scene was progressing. Why was the circle around my chair? It didn't take long to find out.

"Ed! Will you take your place in the chair?" Charley quietly asked.

What was in front of me had no appeal. I didn't want to sit in that chair with all those books around me.

"I don't want to sit in that chair!"

"Why not?"

I didn't know why. My chair, inside that circle, seemed to be some sort of a trap. I knew that sitting in it wouldn't be comfortable. I was confused.

"I don't want to sit there, Charley!"

"Why not?" Charley prodded.

"I don't like it!"

"What don't you like about it, Ed?"

"I don't like the circle around it!"

"What don't you like about the circle? Would you prefer a square?"

"No! I just don't want anything around my chair like that! I don't want any barriers around me!"

What is this guy trying to do to me? I contemplated crossing over the books and sitting on the chair. "Why not?" I asked myself. It's only a circle. It can't hurt me. I decided to cross and sat in the chair. There wasn't much comfort sitting in the chair in that dumb circle. I got up and crossed over to the other side. "I feel much better outside. What else do you want me to do?" I asked Charley sarcastically.

"Anything you want, Ed," he answered kindly.

In great confusion, I crossed over and sat in the chair again. The circle and chair were still creating an uncomfortable feeling within me. Maybe outside was the place for me. Neither place seemed to have any promise of comfort. It didn't seem to matter. Whether I was inside or outside, the circle was creating terrible feelings. It was nothing but a circle. There was no question about that, but the feeling it was creating was another thing.

"Charley! The only thing I want to do is to kick that circle out of the room!"

"Be my guest!" Charley said. "Do it!"

Thoughts of Claudia under the blanket came to my mind. Is this what she experienced? Was this the process leading to anger? I walked over to the books quietly, picked them up and piled them neatly along the side of my chair and sat down.

"I'm not going to kick those books out of this room," I said slowly and with deliberate intent.

There was a long pause. I shifted nervously in my chair once again.

Charley spoke, "Your time is up, Ed. You did a good job. You shared valuable experiences that were informative. That information will help me to understand where you're coming from. I thank you for that, Ed."

"Charley, I know my time is up, but I must know what that circle really means."

"It's a matter of boundaries and limits, Ed," Charley explained. "The circle represents your boundary. By removing the circle you got rid of your boundary. You therefore had no limits. That's where you are now, without limits."

"But what does 'no limits' mean?" I asked.

"You evidently went to a university ill-prepared and used secondary gains to hide those limits," Charley said. "Unfortunately you were not pre ..."

I interrupted, "Charley, I still don't understand what you mean by secondary gains. Would you go over this information just one more time for me?"

Charley paused, rubbed his beard, and answered, "Ed, when one has pain or is ill, the primary gain is to relieve that pain or illness and to feel better. Secondary gains are unconsciously or subconsciously exactly what you did with school. You received your primary gain and also received a secondary gain. You weren't doing this deliberately or planning it. You weren't aware of the connection."

This was all too much for my brain to absorb. I sat deeper into my chair, wishing it would absorb all of me.

"Getting back to what I was saying," Charley continued. "Unfortunately, you were ill-prepared and ill-advised for university studies. The pressures caused by not liking school, trying to satisfy your parents, and knowing you were flunking, created exorbitant tensions within you. Our society does not teach boundaries and limits. Ed, I'm really sorry. We have gone beyond your time and must stop now. I would like to continue this next time."

I could feel the empathy and compassion in his words. How was I going to sort all this out?

I screamed so everyone would hear, "I hate my body!"

16

I CAN'T

An education program, an out-trip, or free time could be this afternoon's activities. The choice was ours. We could attend them, or have the afternoon to ourselves. I chose the education class. Only six patients attended this class. Three more went on the out-trip, which was a walk to the mall. The others just didn't want to do anything, as so often was the case.

The education class met in the activities room. We seated ourselves at a table. Our counselor, Susan, was already there, waiting for us. When we were all settled, Susan asked what we wanted to talk about.

Archie said, in his usual negative way, "I have a few words I would like to say." His voice was raspy and hoarse. "I can't understand how people can go on those out-trips with so much pain in their bodies. I'm sure not going to do that trip. I couldn't stand going to the mall in my condition. No, sir."

Marion completely ignored Archie and went on in another vein to Ethal asking her, "How come you have your pills mashed in orange juice? I've never seen anyone do that before. What a mess!"

Ethal, our constant latecomer, grew pink in the face with anger, replying, "I can't swallow pills or capsules whole. I just can't do it. They get stuck in my throat. You do it your way, I'll do it my way."

My favorite comment was made by an extremely plump woman, a newcomer to the group. She filled the chair completely and spilled over the sides as she spoke, "I can't stand the food in this hospital. I just can't get what I order from the menu. I'll be glad to go home where I can eat what I want."

I wanted to tell her that she was on a one thousand-calorie diet; I knew what she was on because it was the same as mine. Pastries and ice cream were not allowed. But I refrained from doing it. I always tried hard to be polite to people. Someone else wailed, "I can't do anything because it always hurts so much." It was Marjorie—she spends as much time in her bed as she can get away with.

They were becoming complete bores. I wanted to holler out at them that this type of thing was not helpful. This was not education. In fact, this was destructive. I wanted to scream at them. Couldn't they think of anything else to talk about? What kind of an education was this? Susan listened attentively to the interaction. She remained her sweet looking self. Was she bored also? If she was bored, it didn't show. I wondered.

Finally, Susan spoke. "I have a great idea. Let's play a game!" Everyone there, except for me, managed to groan and make derogatory remarks, but Susan maintained her pleasing countenance and said, "I think you'll like it. It could be interesting." She took a pad of paper that was on the table and gave each one of us a sheet. We managed to gather up enough pens and pencils for each other. The patients were giving each other wry looks, as they might have done if they were in grade school.

When we were ready and the grumbling had stopped, Susan said, "On the top of the sheet, write in capital letters, 'I CAN'T.'"

I did as she asked.

"Now, under that heading write five items you can't do. Refrain from writing that you can't fly like a bird, or jump as high as a kangaroo. Nor can you run as fast as a speeding bullet. Don't write any impossibilities."

That was no problem for me. I began writing. My list of, 'I cant's' poured onto the paper.

"Has everyone written the five items?" she asked.

We all nodded.

"Do I have a volunteer to read their list?"

"I will!" Marion said, and immediately began reading.

"1. I can't stop biting my nails.

2. I can't do carpentry work.

3. I can't get my wardrobe together.

4. I can't plan ahead.

5. I can't save money."

"Good! That's very good. Anyone else?" Susan asked.

I volunteered.

"1. I can't do the 12 laps that equal a mile.

2. I can't get rid of my pain.

3. I can't quit smoking.

4. I can't lose forty pounds.

5. I can't get along with my daughter."

The others took their turns.

"Now," Susan said, "here is another piece of paper." She passed them out.

"I want you to write on the top of this page, 'I WON'T', again, in capital letters."

I did that. This all seemed very silly to me. Susan appeared to be studying our faces.

"Now, I want you to take the five items you can't do and write them under the new, 'I WON'T.'"

I thought Susan must be wacky. What was she trying to do? Find out if we can write? I was becoming irritated. Maybe the out-trip would have been a better idea for me.

Susan said, "Instead of having, 'I can't stop biting my nails, you will now have, 'I won't stop biting my nails.' Do you all understand?"

We nodded. More wry faces, more deprecating looks, one to the other.

I started to make the substitutions. This didn't seem like much of an education program. There must be a better way to help me deal with my pain. What was written on my sheet didn't relate to getting rid of it at all. I followed her instructions, totally bored, just going through the motions of making the changes. I wrote:

"1. I won't do the 12 laps that equal a mile."

While writing it a strange feeling began to creep over me.

"2. I won't ... get rid of ... my pain ..."

The feeling was growing worse. What was happening inside of me?

"3. I ... won't ... quit ... smoking."

I could feel some kind of connection. I wasn't quite sure what it was. The 'I can't' and the 'I won't' seemed to have opposite meanings. What was it? I was so puzzled ...

"4. I ... won't ... lose ... forty ... pounds ...

"5. I ... won't ... get ... along ... with ... my ... daughter ..."

Oh, my God, I thought. I won't get along with my daughter. Things began to fit in neatly. 'I can't' really means, 'I won't'. That means I can do anything I want. 'I won't' get along with my daughter struck home. It was a revelation to me!

Susan was very clever. There was so much of the, 'I can't' going on when we first came into the room that it became obnoxious. She used that opportunity to play the game on us. The game was an enlightening one. A lesson was learned. I waited to see how the others reacted.

"Who wants to volunteer to read?" she asked.

Marion quickly said, "I will!" and began reading:

"1. I won't stop biting my nails.

2. I won't do carpentry work.

3. I won't get my wardrobe together.

4. I won't plan ahead.

5. I won't save money."

"How do you feel about the change?" Susan asked Marion.

"I don't feel anything different. I still can't stop biting my nails, and I can't do any of the other things either. I don't know what you hope to prove with this silly game."

Susan didn't answer Marion, but continued with, "Is there anyone else who will offer to read their list of, 'I WON'T'?"

The lesson seemed okay, but what about my interpretation of it? Marion didn't see anything different in it. Maybe my thoughts about it were wrong. The risk involved in reading my list appealed to me. Then a strong urge came over me to share what I had learned.

"I'll read mine," I said. "But first, I have to tell you something. I must tell you what this exercise revealed to me. My 'cant's' were a cover-up for what 'I won't' do. Susan, you want us to know from this exercise that anything can be done within limits. Yes, it is easier for me to say 'I can't' when what I really mean is, 'I won't'. When I use 'I can't', it lets me off the hook. I don't have to try anymore.

I began reading my 'I wont's.'

When I got to, 'I won't get along with my daughter,' tears filled my eyes, and my throat became very hoarse. I had trouble speaking. The lesson I had learned became clear to me right now. Eventually, after I had pulled myself together, I said to the class, "I won't ... get along ... with my daughter."

I waited for some feedback.

Nothing came from the group. Then Susan remarked, "Ed, you said it beautifully. You learned the lesson well."

The education program was over. There were going to be some changes in me. I was going to learn. All these years, I couldn't get along with my daughter. Such a waste of time ... The tears again filled my eyes. They felt good this time. Suddenly, the responsibility was all mine!

17

LENA

I did it. I really did it! I wrote one hundred sentences about wanting to quit smoking. I got up, walked to the doorway of my room, stood there, eyed both ends of the hallway, and lit up a cigarette. What a waste of time! I looked at my watch. My nine o'clock body massage was fast approaching, and at least that would not be a waste.

While standing there, my favorite aria from the "Pearl Fishers" began to tenor and baritone out of my radio. Goose-bumps formed on the back of my neck and continued down my back. I loved that aria. Why had it come on now? The timing couldn't have been better. The aria seemed like a reward for the one hundred sentences. I thought of what I had written. The words I had used to form sentences had no convincing power in them at all. My penmanship was poor. The sentence structure was messy. It was obvious that those sentences were not going to help me quit smoking. Still, even though writing a hundred sentences was a boring chore, I had done it. I wondered if I would do it again. I wondered if it would do any good.

My thoughts were interrupted by a commotion down the hallway. A stretcher was being rolled out of the elevator by two aides and was headed toward me. The stretcher was carrying a new patient, who appeared as a great hulk. I wondered if that was the way I looked being moved on stretchers from one area to another when I was in hospitals. Brain, we must lose weight. If I told myself one hundred times would that help me lose weight? Moaning and groaning could be heard as the stretcher rolled by. Its rider's back was to me, but I could tell the body was female by the long hair and the tone of the moaning. She was rolled into a room a few doors down.

I checked my watch. It was time to go for my massage. The tenor and baritone had finished the aria, as if it were planned. If the music had meant to fill my being with joyous feelings, it had succeeded. Off I went. I felt lighthearted.

Thoughts about Lena came to mind as I headed slowly down the hall for my massage. I hadn't realized before that Lena was more than just my masseuse. Mal informed me yesterday that she was also my counselor, and I could discuss anything that bothered me.

Many things were puzzling me. I needed some answers. Maybe I could ask Lena. I had witnessed two scenes demonstrating violent anger. One was directed at the water, where the patient was beating the water. The other, a blanket trap. Why? I'd experienced excruciating pain when Mal spoke, which ceased only when she finished. Also, during my constellation session, why couldn't I raise my hand? Then to be told I was dominated by women! What did this all mean?

It was time. My shyness, my lack of confidence, had to be put aside. I needed to talk with Lena.

Once in the massage room, I greeted Lena. She always replied in a positive manner that I wished I could master. She made me feel good. Her sincerity in whatever she said was obvious, just like her massages. I undressed, got on the table as usual, and began telling her about Agnes.

Lena's Swedish accent interrupted with, "Ed, did you know you walked in here without dragging your leg?"

"WHAT?" I said.

She repeated, "You walked in here without any sign of a limp in your left leg. Amazing!"

I got off the table holding my towel and started walking. I stared at my legs as I walked across the floor. I looked up and I looked down. I couldn't believe it! She was right. I wasn't dragging my leg. Dumbstruck, I looked at Lena. "What happened?"

Lena smiled at me. "Just what I said, Ed."

"Lena, this is unbelievable!" I stared at her. "Is all this in my head?"

"No, Ed, this is really happening to you. You are making progress. Enjoy it and don't stop."

I decided then and there to share what I had done before coming to see her. I sat back on the table and blurted out to her, "Lena, you won't believe this. Before I came here, I wrote one hundred times that I was going to quit smoking. When I finished, I got up, went to my doorway and lit up a cigarette. Then my favorite aria from the "Pearl Fishers" played. It rewarded me for what I'd done, and now I've come here ... not dragging my leg. Is this another reward? What does all this mean?"

Lena answered, "Ed, rejoice in the feeling you have right now. Just stay in it. Don't think of anything else."

"Oh, Lena," my voice was soft and full, "I wish my wife were here, so I could share this with her. I would give her a big hug and never let go."

"Ed, I'll be her surrogate," Lena said.

I went to her and hugged her with one arm, while the other held the towel. It was the first time I had ever done that to anyone but my wife. I choked up again and this time I cried. I wasn't too worried about it either.

Pulling myself together, I returned my hulk to the table and waited for the coconut oil to soothe my skin. The oil began doing its magic, helped along by those healing hands that no words could describe. All my aches and pains were vanishing. She was rubbing and rubbing. No pain existed at that moment.

Lena interrupted my ecstasy and said, "Ed, my hands are feeling some good vibrations coming from you." Her magical rubbing, in its rhythm, continued. "I would like to attach a suggestion to those vibrations. Would you like to hear it?"

"I sure would."

"Add this to your attempt to quit smoking," Lena said, while never missing a beat in her stroking.

"My feeling is that you will write the quit smoking sentences again." Rub, rub, rub, her hands performing on my back. "When you're through and ready to light up a cigarette, look at it first. Tell the cigarette you are going to stop smoking. This part is very important. Let your brain hear the words. When your brain hears the words it will react to your demand, provided the action of quitting goes along with it. It is possible you will only stop for a short while, but that is a good beginning."

My voice was choked with thickness from the pleasure of the rubbing. I had to force myself to ask her, "Are you saying that before I light up a cigarette, I should tell my brain that I'm going to quit smoking, not in my thoughts, but verbally, so that my brain can hear it?"

"Yes, and you must stop smoking the moment after you have told your brain that you are going to do so.

"That sounds very difficult to do."

"Yes, it is difficult to stop smoking, but you have already put that desire into motion. All you need now is a little more push, and you'll quit."

I raised my head awkwardly to look in her eyes. "Lena, I'm going to quit smoking. I promise you that."

"Okay, Ed." She smiled. "I believe you. Now let's get on with the massage."

I allowed those hands to send me into another world, but as I was drifting away, once again I was interrupted with, "Ed, what were you trying to say when you came in?" Lena said it, so I didn't mind postponing my journey. I started to tell her about Agnes and not being able to raise my hand to stop her from advancing toward me.

"Yes, I know," Lena said.

Dumbfounded, I asked, "How did you know?"

"Ed, I'm your counselor, remember?"

"What exactly does that mean?"

"Whatever happens during any of your sessions is discussed later with those who need to know. Your experiences must be shared with others assigned to you, so that each of us is aware of what's going on. How else can we help you?"

At first I didn't like the idea of having my experiences discussed with others, but Lena was able to set my mind at ease. She kept on applying the oil with the soothing strokes that helped my blood flow into all areas of my body.

"Ed, do you feel comfortable talking with me?"

"I am comfortable, but I guess I don't want to bother you with my problems."

"Your problems, Ed, are mine too. That's why I'm your counselor. I'm here to help you sort out those problems. Do you understand that?"

"Not really. I just don't understand all this. I always thought the doctors were the ones to help me. I know you're not a doctor, and I don't know how you can help. You don't do any operations, or give out medicines. Your massages always make me feel good, but they only get rid of my pain for the moment. How can you help me?"

"By simply talking," Lena answered. "The more you talk, the more comfortable you become, and the more conflicts you will confront."

"Conflicts?" I repeated, my head cradled on the mat between my arms. "I don't have any conflicts."

"Everyone has conflicts, Ed," Lena said. "I have my own, and I recognize them. It's recognizing them that is important, and how you deal with them."

Surprised, I said, "You have conflicts?"

"Yes, I do," Lena answered. "The Pain Unit knows that your conflicts are creating tensions that are driven into your back as pain. Like I have said before, your back is like a washboard. Those conflicts that you are allowing to surface can lead us into new avenues of approach. We have all the facilities and the means to help you. Right now, your willingness to talk is one of those avenues. Talking is very helpful."

"You're talking over my head," I said. "What do you mean by new avenues? How can talking be helpful?"

"Ed, talking creates an openness. It leads to an awareness and an intimacy that you can share with those who are willing to help you. You are now aware of your constellation. If you hadn't talked, you wouldn't have known about it. Now, your awareness will allow you to sort it out. It's a great beginning."

Lena finished the massage and went outside the curtains, allowing me to get dressed.

While dressing, I raised my voice and said, "I'm at a complete loss. I'm not at all familiar with what you're talking about. I was brought up to let a doctor treat and prescribe medicine for any of my illnesses. Now you're saying talking will help."

"I know that what I am saying is difficult for you to understand. You're looking for that quick cure which comes from taking a pill, and it's gone," Lena said. "Your pain is far more complicated than that. Consider how many operations you've had. Your pain is still there. The only choice you have is to learn to live with it. In order to do that, you must use the basic approach of talking."

I finished dressing and made sure to start walking slowly so that I did not experience that first near fall. "I'm still confused about the talking bit," I said.

"Ed, look what you have already revealed: your family constellation; you weren't able to stop Agnes from bowling over you; you were always sent out to play; you have no limits; your rigid Catholic family background. These are important points for Charley to work on. Charley now has something concrete. If, for example, your constellation is connected to your pain, Charley will find that out. Then, he can treat it."

I interrupted, "Just exactly who is Charley, and what is there about him that makes him always seem so wonderful to me?"

Lena answered, "Charley is a psychomotor therapist. He's very dedicated to his profession. You'll not find a better psychotherapist. Charley is capable of getting in touch with your feelings. What you feel, he feels. It's like he gets inside of you and you both become one. He doesn't allow any biases to get in his way. That's why you then begin to speak freely and easily. He starts with your history, right from the beginning to the present. Look what he's already brought out. Your constellation, promises that weren't kept, the great amount of attention given to your brother, the awfully scary way you learned how to swim, and other things that you have dealt with that we don't know about yet. You have positive strengths that need to be reinforced, so you can deal with other conflicts that will surface. Those conflicts are definitely there. As I have already said this is a great beginning for you. Right now we must end. My time is up. But there will be more."

Lena smiled, placed her hand on my arm and said, "You're going to make it, Ed."

"See you tomorrow morning," I said, and left. Her last words "You're going to make it" rang in my mind. I didn't even know what I was supposed to make. It was a good thing my legs knew where to go. My mind and brain didn't.

18

GESTALT THERAPY

At 9 o'clock, on alternating Saturday mornings, sessions of Gestalt Therapy were scheduled. It was mandatory for all Pain Unit patients to attend them. The sessions concluded at midday. Those patients who were allowed to go home for the weekend did.

At one of the Gestalt Therapy sessions, I was asked if I had any fears. I gave a list that included a fear of my back being cancerous, being afraid to go anywhere, and a major fear of not being able to speak in front of a group. I had told how my body tightened up, and my words slurred, and I couldn't articulate them. I just couldn't speak to a group.

Today is Saturday morning once again, and Gestalt Therapy is scheduled. I entered the dining room where the sessions were usually held. My only thought was to hurry, so that I could sit on the closest chair. I either wanted to lie down or sit down. Hurry and sit, hurry and lie down—my whole life was one big rush for one or the other.

The chairs were arranged in a circle. Some patients were already sitting and talking. I immediately took the closest chair. I didn't want to walk any farther. I imagined others felt the same as I did.

Breathing heavily and listening to the words flying back and forth, I writhed in my chair. The same words from the previous sessions blared again, all related to complaints. To anyone else it must have been sheer boredom.

"Did you see what they gave me for breakfast?" said one overfilled body.

"Why won't they give me what I ordered?" cried another.

"They always change my menu. I never get what I check off!" another accused.

"I don't know why the doctor won't give me more pain medication" was a habitual complaint.

"The pain is worse. It's much worse since I have been here!" another whined.

"Did you hear what the doctor said to me during rounds? He said I don't need any pain medication. What does he think I should do? Lie here and suffer?" moaned one who always needed medication of some kind.

Then, unbelievably, a voice said, "The pool water was only at 92 degrees yesterday! It's supposed to be at 96 degrees. It was too cold!"

I couldn't understand the complaints these people had. All I wanted to do was to get rid of my pain. I was also afraid to complain. When I was growing up, complaining wasn't allowed, especially at home. We were made to do what we were told, and we could not say a word in defense. I never complained. It wasn't done!

Our therapist was young and very thin. He had jet black hair and a matching black beard. His name was Mike. He wore dungarees and a matching dark shirt. I often wondered why most male therapist wore beards or long mustaches. It probably helped them to hide their facial language. A patient couldn't see what the therapist's face was saying behind his beard. I wondered how a female therapist handled the situation.

As he was greeting us, my thoughts went back to the last session. I hope he doesn't call on me this time. I had closed the last session by revealing a fear of facing and speaking to groups of people. Whenever I had something to say to a large group, I got tongue-tied. A cold sweat overtook my body. I just wanted to run away. As I was thinking about it, a voice echoed, saying, "Ed! Last time we closed with your fear ..."

"Oh, no." I went numb. "Why me? Why is he calling on me again?" I thought angrily. The pain began tormenting my back. My leg couldn't have felt worse.

"Ed! Would you like to continue where you left off last time?"

"I don't think so," I replied, showing some annoyance that he had chosen me.

"Why don't you think so?" He insisted on knowing.

"I guess I don't feel comfortable this minute. I can't start the discussion," I stated hesitantly.

"That's all right, Ed. Maybe you'll feel like it later."

Why does he want to come back to me? There are so many here!

Then in a flash he was. It seemed like only a minute had passed.

"Ed, are you comfortable now? Would you like to continue?" he asked.

I answered reluctantly, "I guess so."

"You said you have a fear of speaking in a group."

"Yes I do," I answered.

"What actually does happen to you when you are in a group and you want to say something?"

"I get very uncomfortable."

"Tell me what happens," he urged.

Since I was in a large group at that moment, I began to feel thoroughly uncomfortable. The pain was intense. My breathing was shallow; I was panting. The sweat was beginning to pour out of me; beads were lining my forehead. I really wanted to run away. I decided that I should explain exactly what was going on with me at this very moment. Maybe that would be helpful.

"I get very uncomfortable," I whispered in a gruff, barely audible voice. It sounded like I was moaning.

He couldn't hear me. "Tell me again what happens," he urged again, gently, but insistently.

"I don't know!" That was the standard pat-answer I used for every question when I was uncomfortable. "I don't know! I just get very uncomfortable. I feel like I want to run away." I barely whispered my response to him.

"What did you say Ed? I can't hear you."

In a slightly louder voice I said, "I don't know. I just get uneasy."

"Fine, Ed, I know how you feel. You are in a group now. There are twenty people here. I want you to tell us what you feel physically, what is going through your mind, and anything else that comes to you. Feel free to say whatever you think of. Don't try to remember what happened during past sessions. Stick with this one. Tell me what is happening now."

Taking a deep breath and closing my eyes, I said, "I'm afraid."

What are you afraid of?" Mike coaxed.

"I'm afraid that others are watching, and they'll think what I'm saying is silly."

"Go on," he encouraged. "Try it."

At this juncture, I felt all sweaty. I had butterflies in my stomach. Inside, all I wanted was to get the hell out of there.

I said, "I have difficulty verbalizing the words that come to my mind. I feel what I am going to say won't be understood. I guess I don't want anyone here to think I'm weak. At this very moment, I'm feeling insecure. I'm having difficulty saying it out loud."

My God! What am I doing? How can anyone admit to a group that they're insecure? This is terrible. I think I'm going out of my mind. I stopped. I realized what I was thinking. My eyes shot up to Mike.

"You're doing it, Ed," he said. "You're doing just fine." His voice hinted of empathy and kindness.

"I am?"

"Tell me what else you're afraid of," prodded Mike.

"Well, I'm afraid to say something that may offend someone. I may provoke an argument I can't handle. I'm afraid it may not come out in the right way. Then, if I'm questioned, how will I answer? What would I do? When I have to supply some kind of an answer I find myself agreeing and nodding my head and agreeing some more, whether I agree or not. My favorite words are 'yes, yes'! That would kill me to do that now."

I bellowed, "RIGHT NOW I FEEL AWFUL!". I stopped. There was a pause. It was an everlasting pause.

Mike broke the silence. "Ed, I want you to do an experiment for me."

In desperation I said, "Another experiment?" I was now remembering the last one I'd done.

"Yes, an experiment," he said.

"What kind of an experiment?" I wanted to know. I needed to know.

Warmth and kindness glowed from Mike's person. "It's one that will help you. I'm sure it will help." I could feel myself wanting to respond to his warmth.

I gulped, swallowed, cleared my throat one more time, shifted positions in my chair and replied, "Let's hear it."

"I want you to say something to each group member that you think would be offensive to them. Start with the first person on your left. Then I want you to do the same thing to the next person on the left and then continue with the remainder of the group."

"YOU WHAT! ARE YOU KIDDING ME?" I didn't know where the sound came from, but I bellowed at him again.

"NO ...You're NOT KIDDING," I shouted, sensing through his bearded face that he was serious. "You really want me to do that?"

"Yes, I want you to do it. Please, Ed, try hard. I want you to tell them something, only one thing, that you do not like about them, the way they act or the way they look, or even the way they sleep." Mike was tenderhearted; his warm heart was noticeable in his voice.

I swallowed hard. The lump that had formed in my throat was hard to get rid of. "He must be nuts!" I said to myself. The tension was back and the rigidity in my spine was terrible. The pain was awful! I was in agony!

"Go ahead, Ed, please try," I heard Mike say.

I looked to my left. I searched the faces of the patients before me. I began to shrink. All the fears I had revealed swelled up inside of me. "NO! I can't do what you ask."

"Ed, you can," he tried to assure me. "You can."

I thought of some of the skills we had learned in order to handle just a such situation. Take a deep breath when you are experiencing such discomforts. I did. I took one deep breath, exhaled, and then another and another. I closed my eyes and sucked in all the air I could. I exhaled and made sure that all the air came out. I did this for what seemed an eternity.

I was stalling and I knew it. The group knew I was stalling. Mike knew I was stalling.

All at once, for some unknown reason, courage cleared away the fears and negative feelings I was experiencing. I could hear my voice telling Jim, "I don't like the color of your shirt."

Startled, at what I'd just said to Jim, I turned and looked at Mike, "Is this what you want me to do?"

"Yes, Ed, that's exactly what I want you to do."

Turning back to Jim, I repeated, "I don't like the color of your shirt at all. I would never wear it." I then turned to Ethal, "Do you always have to be late for the group meetings?" I was beginning to enjoy what I was doing when I said to Marion, "I don't like women who smoke and I wish you would stop complaining about the massages. They're good for you." I then looked at Mal. "Mal, can't you wear colorful clothes that match?" Again, I spoke, "Marty, you're always sarcastic, no matter what the situation."

The patients in the group sat there and listened to what I said about them, and said absolutely nothing. They were like zombies, just staring at me.

What am I doing, I wondered. I paused and then continued with my task, saying to Mike, who was next, "I don't like beards. I think you're hiding behind it. You won't let your true feelings come out. I feel they hide something more than just your face."

To the following patient I said, "You always complain about the menu. But you always say someone changes it on you. You order bacon, butter, sugar, salt, and all the items your diet is supposed to restrict. You know when you order them they will never be given to you. Still you whine about it daily."

I had begun to feel at ease and realized what was happening to me. I was becoming stronger, more sure of myself.

Mary was next. My mind went blank. I paused, looked at her, and scrutinized her face. Maybe I could complain about her hair, her smoking habits or her blouse. But no, nothing came out of my mouth. I could not form negative comments about Mary. I concentrated harder, but still no words came forth. I turned and looked at Mike. "I can't say anything bad about her, no matter how hard I try my mind goes blank. I don't know why."

"Ed, you are doing fine, just fine. Continue on and something will come," he said reassuringly.

I tried, but my thoughts kept going back to Mary. "I know I like her—not the way I like my wife—but I do like her very much. She's a nice person. Maybe that's why I can't say anything bad about her."

My eyes traveled around the group and rested on Mary's face. I wanted desperately to say something negative about her, but nothing would form in my mind. Whenever I tried, my mind went empty. A frustrating silence filled it. I looked at Mary once again. It was no use. I could not hurt her. "That's it, except for Mary," I said to Mike. "The only thing that bothers me now is the turmoil my mind is in about Mary."

"Ed, you did a great job," Mike reassured me. "How do you feel now?"

"I feel relieved that it's all over. It was a difficult exercise; I don't know if any of my friends in the group will ever like me again, but I now understand the need for an experience like that.

"Mike, Mary is still a puzzle to me. Every time I looked at her, I couldn't think of anything to say. Not a word would come to my lips."

He looked at me. I could see a smile in his eyes as he asked, "Ed, what is your wife's name?"

I answered, "Mary. MARY! That's my wife's name. No wonder!"

"Yes, Ed, that's why. You have demonstrated the Gestalt mechanism to overcome fears or phobias. The more the mechanism is used, the stronger you become. The most effective way to relieve your fears or phobias is to confront them head-on. You did that." Mike took a deep breath and sighed, "That's it for this morning. I wish you all well. Whoever is going home for the weekend, have yourself a good one." He sat back in his chair and seemed relieved.

I left and headed for my room to prepare for Mary who was coming to drive me home for the weekend. She was already there waiting for me. I hugged her, and said, "I'll be ready in a minute." I gathered what was necessary and left with her by my side.

Inside the car, I dominated the talk with what had happened at the Gestalt Therapy. She was intrigued. As we approached our home my pain began to increase. "Got to get rid of this car," I complained. "Right now I hurt really bad."

"We will," Mary agreed. "We'll talk to Jim Darling over at the Buick place and ask him find a good used car, one that we can afford."

"Okay," I said.

The weekend was great but I had a lot of pain that minimized my activities. On the way back to the Pain Unit I noticed how my pain diminished. When I got there I was pretty comfortable. What was going on?

19

THE KITCHEN

It was pool time—my favorite time. Off I went; I donned my bathing suit and immersed my body in the pool's warm water. What I liked best was releasing my anger into the water, and the relaxed state it created.

I was standing in the middle of the pool while the other patients straggled in. I began to swing my arms like wings, hitting the water with them. The force from the swing created large waves. I swung and swung and swung. It felt good. I could hear, "Go ahead Ed, hit it harder!" I did just that. I hit it harder and harder. As the other patients entered the pool, they began to join me.

What turbulence we created in that pool! Some water hit the walls. Cheryl, smiling, was standing next to the walls and had to scamper away to avoid being soaked.

I swam to the other side of the pool and stretched my arms out on top of the coping. I started to kick the water. I kicked and kicked and kicked, until I was at the point of absolute exhaustion. Nearly all the patients were either kicking or hitting the water. Finally, I had to stop, as did the others. I had used up all my energy. I was exhausted.

Cheryl seemed delighted, brushing away some of the water that had splashed her. She was laughing at us as she spoke, "I think after that demonstration, we should immediately go into our exercises." She paused for a moment, looked around, put her hands on her hips, and raised her voice saying, "Let's take up our positions against a wall."

We did as she directed, took our positions, got comfortable, and automatically began taking deep breaths, which was the beginning of our exercise. Cheryl talked us through our usual pool exercise routine. We needed to do each exercise six times: raising a leg in front of our body, then out to the side; tilting our body back and forth to the right and left of each side; the pelvic tilt; raising a knee and grabbing it with both hands and pulling it up further; standing on our toes; raising each arm in a circle forward and backward; neck circles in one direction then the opposite; crossing our legs and twisting our torso to the right and to the left.

What surprised me most was the ease with which I was able to do the exercises in the water. It took no effort at all. I guessed doing them in the water did make it easier.

We heard Cheryl say, "Spread your arms atop the coping, close your eyes, don't allow any thoughts to come in. Just feel your body relax." Cheryl waited a minute or so and said, "Open your eyes, know where you are, and begin to move your body." Very slowly, very emphatically Cheryl stated, "Everyday in every way you are going to feel better and better. That's it. You're dismissed."

I thought that was the fastest fifty minutes I had ever spent. As we were getting out of the pool Cheryl shouted, "Groups A and C! When you come to P. T. bring along a jacket. It's cold outside."

I got dressed and headed for my room to get ready for dinner. The noon meal was the dinner at the rehab, whereas the evening meal was more of a lunch.

I was feeling good and began reflecting on my accomplishments at the Pain Unit. I was still losing nearly a pound a day. I was now walking six laps along the periphery of the second floor. Another six laps and I would reach my goal of one mile. I couldn't believe what I had accomplished. My back was still painful, but I was able to keep going. All my exercises had doubled, with two miles on the bicycle. The first time I'd pedaled the bike for such a short distance that I couldn't get the mileage to register.

It came as a big surprise the day I was able to bend down and pick things up off the floor. My colitis didn't act up at all anymore. Best of all, I'd lost my limp. Strange. I couldn't remember which leg was limping.

Each day I would do one of the relaxation exercises, sometimes twice. I would switch from Biofeedback (raising the leg, etc.) to Think of the Top of Your Head and Tighten It, and then work down to the feet. I always felt better than good after the exercises. What a gift!

I had my dinner, went to my room, grabbed my jacket, and headed for PT and Cheryl. Today was going to be shopping day. Cheryl was going to point out some things to think about while shopping. She mentioned a study that was done of men standing at a bar, and the length of time they would stand there. Some men could stand at a bar for hours. How could they stand that long and not feel some discomfort? The study showed that any bar that had a footrail made it easier for the patron to stand there for a long time. The footrail was the key. Placing the foot on the rail relieved the pressure on the spine, allowing one to stand for a long time.

Cheryl suggested that when we went shopping, and we had to wait in line at a checkout counter, that we place a foot on the bottom part of the shopping cart to relieve the pressure on our spines. Also, when picking anything up from the bottom shelf we should squat and not bend.

We arrived at the supermarket and went through the routine of shopping and following her instructions. I had already known about the squatting rather than bending. What really surprised me though was the waiting in line at the checkout. I did what Cheryl suggested and could immediately feel the pain decrease in my back when I put my foot on the bottom of the shopping cart. When I checked out and paid for my items, I felt more comfortable. It really did work.

We got through the checkout and returned to the Pain Unit. It was late, and I had to rush for my next activity, psychodrama. I was only now beginning to realize the importance of psychodrama. This acting out the part of a troubling situation with a different person was intriguing. We were able to see the problem immediately within the scene and notice how we came across. Seeing how one appeared to others sometimes revealed an odd behavior that could easily be understood and corrected. It was a great method for solving problems.

I returned to my room and hung up my jacket, then I went to the activities room where the psychodrama was to be held. Everyone from my group was there. I couldn't help noticing, though, that not one of them had gone to the shopping lesson.

Ms. Rede came over to me, smiling, with her arms outstretched, ready for a hug. I thought of Susan during the Sensory Awareness class, walked right into her arms, and hugged her. It felt good.

"That's a good hug, Ed," she said.

"Yes!" I answered, tossing my head back to look at her, "Am I getting better at it?"

Ms. Rede smiled, nodded her head in approval, and enthusiastically said, "You sure are!"

We sat in our seats. Ms. Rede began to explain, once again, what psychodrama was about. After a few moments, Archie seemed to have something on his mind that couldn't wait. He interrupted with, "I don't understand why my wife always snaps at me when I bring up a legitimate complaint. It never fails. She'll come home from work and place her bag, or whatever she has in her hands, on the nearest counter or chair. If there were a dish of dirt there, her stuff would go right on top of it. If I complain about it, she automatically yells back with, 'You ALWAYS tell me what I do wrong! You never, ever think to tell me what I do that's right!'

Now, Ms. Rede," Archie's voice oozed with sarcasm, "show me with your psychodrama how I should handle that!"

"I'm so glad you brought that up. That's an ideal subject for psychodrama." Ms. Rede clapped her hands with elation. She was a jolly type who always had energy to spare. She was happy all the time. She found something good in everything we did. I found when I was with her that I, too, felt happy. I smiled a lot, it seemed.

Ms. Rede said, "We couldn't ask for a better subject. Ed, will you be Archie?"

I didn't answer. "Why is she asking me?" I thought.

"Who wants to be Ed's wife?" Ms. Rede's words bubbled from her smiling mouth.

"I will!" Mal volunteered.

"Good," Ms. Rede replied. She then turned to face me and asked again, "Ed, will you be Archie?"

I shrank down in my chair, just a bit. I wanted to please her, but I really did not want to do it. I was on the spot. I reluctantly said, "Ok, I will."

"Good, Ed, I'm glad you agreed. Archie will be able to see exactly how he comes across by watching you." Ms. Rede then turned to Archie and asked, "Archie will you describe what happened in your kitchen, so that Mal and Ed can get an idea of what they are acting out?"

"Ok," Archie answered. "The back door of my house leads into the kitchen. There is an isle in the center, with four stools. The seats turn in any direction. Two stools are at each long side of the isle. This is our general eating area. The stove is set diagonally to the right of the back door. There are cabinets set on the floor with countertops, and others are secured to the wall all around the kitchen—plenty of room to temporarily place anything that needs to be set down.

Archie turned to me and said, "Ed, you will be standing at the stove cooking some soup. Remember that you had left your recipe book open, so you can follow the instructions, at that end of the isle closest to the back door.

Archie finished my instructions, turned to Mal, and continued, "Mal, you will have just traveled thirty miles in some horrendous traffic. You will be tired. Even your voice will be weary. You will open the door and say, 'Hi! What did you do today?'"

He turned to me again and said, "Ed, when she walks into the kitchen and greets you, you will sound gruff. You will become angry ... Okay! That's it.,"

I beckoned, "Let me rehearse this a moment."

I was not at all sure how to start. I bumbled along trying to imagine the kitchen—where things were, what to do, and what to say when Mal came home from work. Hesitatingly, I tried to start talking. I couldn't. Nothing would come out of my mouth. I stopped. I cleared my throat a couple of times and looked at Ms. Rede. I nodded my head no, hoping she would cancel this one. Instead she nodded, yes, and smiled encouragingly for me to continue. I wasn't very happy. I felt like I was only wasting time. After looking at her smiling, round face, filled with energy and enthusiasm, I decided I would try once again.

Then I heard, "All right, are you ready?" Ms. Rede asked?

Mal nodded. We began.

I took my position and pretended to be cooking with my back to her. I also pretended to hear the door open. Turning slightly, while continuing to cook, I gave a perfunctory, "Hi."

Mal responded with, "Hi, Ed." There was a slight pause. "What did you do today?"

I answered with great anger. My voice was loud. "What do you mean what did I do today? What the hell can I do, stuck here all the time?" I looked over at my cookbook.

"For Christ sakes, look what you've done. Goddamn it, you put your garbage on top of my recipe."

"I didn't see it," Mal responded in a very small voice—a whine.

"You didn't see it! How can you miss the damn thing? It's right there in front of you!"

"You're doing it again. You're always telling me what I do wrong." Her voice was now trembling.

"Why do you give me so much ammunition to work with?"

"Look, I've had a hard day. The children were awful, and the traffic was horrible." Her voice was choked with anger and tears. She was ready to cry.

"You had a hard day. That is really funny." Sarcasm and derision dripped from my voice as I hollered, "At least you can go out. Look at me. I'd give anything to be able to have your day. I don't want to be here. I don't want to stay here. I hate it here. I hate this reversed roll bit. I hate it! I hate it!"

Nothing could stop me now. I was enraged. I was ready to continue for however long it took.

Mal choked out her words through her tears. "You're always telling me the same thing. Can't you come up with something different? Why are you always picking on me? You're never, ever nice anymore. You seem to have gone away. You're not the same Ed I married." Now Mal was really crying, and I felt a strange feeling come over me.

At this point I stopped. The feelings I was experiencing were frightening me. It was as if I were reliving a scene from home. It had become so real. I no longer felt like I was acting. Mal had made the scene more than real. An overwhelming tiredness came over me, and I had to sit down.

"Are you all right, Ed?" Ms. Rede asked, concerned, putting her arm on my shoulder.

"Yeah, I'm all right. I am just so tired and feel so sad. I want to cry."

"You both did a marvelous job. Just sit back, Ed, while I ask the group to comment on the performance"

There was a long pause. People shifted in their chairs.

"It looked so real," a voice said. "I've never seen anything like it."

"That was great," another voice said.

"Good job. Better than a stage show," continued another voice.

Archie followed with, "Yeah! Boy! Can I relate to that. That's exactly how it happened!"

I sat in the chair, my head down, hands folded between my legs. I was staring at the floor.

I hadn't been acting!

20

THE PILLOW

It was time for my rap session. On my way there, I met Mal in the hallway. She was no longer my guide. Instead, we had become Pain Unit friends. Together, we headed for the room where the session was to be held.

I liked what I saw in Mal. She believed in the Pain Unit. Often, she told me that she had made up her mind to experience everything the Pain Unit had to offer. She accepted what felt comfortable and discarded what didn't. Her arms didn't seem to be any better, but she did admit that her mind and brain were seeing things in a more positive way. Mentally, she felt much better than she had in her pre-Pain Unit days.

I decided to do the same thing. Breaking my old habits wasn't easy. The discomfort and confusion in sorting them out sent pain to my back. I had never been taught to learn about myself before now.

As we walked, Mal spoke about the new patient, Callie, who had been brought in on a stretcher a couple of days ago. Mal said that Callie seemed to feel better and would join our group at the rap session. She warned me not to be surprised at seeing Callie on a stretcher. She also mentioned that Callie would replace Claudia, who had graduated. The group would be evened up.

I told Mal about seeing Callie the morning she had arrived. I had planned to visit her, but never did.

Mal hadn't noticed that I wasn't limping. I asked her if she saw anything different about me. She said she didn't, so I pointed out that I wasn't limping. She couldn't believe it and apologized for not noticing.

Mal said, "It's amazing how our brain reacts, through our eyes and senses, to others who are in severe pain. Back pain is typical. Everyone I know who has a back problem will be limping, dragging a leg, or bent over when they arrive. Ed, you came to the Pain Unit dragging your leg. Then the dragging changed to limping. Now, you're doing neither one. Maybe there is some truth to that business of pain being a learned behavior."

We entered a room that had a couch and chairs already set up to form a neat circle. The hideous couch took up most of the circle. It looked comfortable, but it tortured anyone who had a back problem. Sitting in it was so awkward that I had to look through my knees to see anyone. Trying to rise up out of it was next to impossible for anyone and even worse for a back patient. The couch simply held me in it, with no possibility of moving. It took just one sitting for me to realize that it was utterly useless. When would they make furniture that was suitable for the disabled to get out of easily? I chose a straight, solid, disagreeable chair, but one that was easy to leave when the meeting ended.

The two aides, Agnes and Kay, arrived, greeted us, and took seats next to each other. Then the rest of our group came in and took their places. The couch always filled up first. I couldn't understand why anyone would want to sit in it.

Agnes announced the arrival of the new patient. She said, "Callie will join us in a few moments. She is unable to walk right now. Her back is very painful. She will be brought in on a stretcher."

As soon as these words had been said, the stretcher was rolled in, and some patients got up to make room for it. Agnes waved them off, signifying that they should not move. She announced to the group, "Callie, while on her stretcher, is up high enough to see us all."

Callie was greeted and welcomed. She moaned and said in a whining voice, "I would rather be in my bed. There isn't much room on this stretcher. I'm in awful pain."

Marion whined in sympathy, "What happened?"

Callie's voice seemed filled with confusion. She moaned, "I don't know. I just bent down to tie my shoe. I felt a stabbing pain in my back and couldn't straighten out. An ambulance took me to the hospital where x-rays were taken, other tests were done, and nothing was found to be wrong. The doctors decided to send me here. I don't know why. I never heard of a Pain Unit before. Anyway, here I am."

Mal said in a comforting tone, "The Pain Unit will help you. You wait and see."

Agnes interrupted and said, "O.K., let's get on with the session. Ed. How is your back today?"

I tried to say, "bad today," but it came out garbled. I coughed to clear my throat and started again. "Very bad today," I finally answered. "I'm in great pain now."

"Join us, then. That seems to be the problem with most of us!" Ernie exclaimed.

"I don't have a bad back," Mal broke in. "It's my arms. I have bad arms from those operations." She began rubbing her arms.

"Yes, I have a bad back, too," Shirley complained.

Agnes broke in and said, "Wait a minute! What's this about having a bad back and bad arms? We don't have bad backs or arms. They're not bad! They're injured, diseased, achy, yes, but they're not bad. Let's get rid of that 'bad' business." She glanced around the circle and seemed to be studying our reactions to what she had said.

Her words made no sense to me. I had learned that if something hurt, then the hurt was "bad." Whether the pain was in my arms, my back, or my head, it was "bad."

Agnes explained, "It would be to your advantage to think in positive terms rather than negative ones. When you say 'bad,' your brain hears it as negative and reacts in that mode. If all your 'bads' are painful, that's the signal your brain is getting. It has no choice but to let you feel 'the bad' as pain. When you are positive about things, your brain will give the pain less attention, allowing you to be more comfortable.

The pain may not go away completely, but it may be easier to bear."

Suddenly, something happened to me. Why, I didn't know. I felt a strong desire to unleash, to open my mind. A force was pushing me to tell the group about my problems. I had listened to everyone else's, and now it was my turn. I wanted to do it! There I was, talking and dominating the session. I seemed to have lost my self-consciousness; I was calm for a change. I also noticed that everyone was looking at me. My mouth grew dry. I was nervous and tense, but I talked on anyway. I decided that this was my chance to tell people how I felt. I started by telling the group about the perfunctory attitudes most of the doctors had shown to my back problems.

"I was involved in a car accident. My lawyer told me to go to a certain doctor who knew all the ropes for making a good case against the insurance company. When I got to the doctor's office, without even looking at me, he asked 'Where does it hurt?' I told him and expected a thorough exam. There wasn't one—not even an Xray. There was nothing. He wrote on his pad for a few minutes, then said, 'Okay, you can go now.' He didn't do anything at all and charged $150.00 for the visit. Before I left he said, 'Don't worry. Everything will be all right.' Boy did that bother me!"

"Yeah, I know," said Ernie. "The only thing your doctor wanted was the one hundred and fifty bucks he was getting. Worse though, the insurance company probably paid it, no questions asked."

Shirley spoke. "What bothers me is that these doctors are working with the lawyers, and they act as if they are on the up and up. Wouldn't I like a business like that? How anyone can take money that easily is a mystery to me! It's almost like they are saying, 'Let's make money from those who are suffering.'"

My topic appeared to have awakened the group. They all had something to add to my discouraging stories about doctors, lawyers, and insurance companies.

Kay asked, "Ed, are you saying you don't trust doctors, lawyers, or insurance companies?"

I wasn't allowed to answer. The other patients broke in with their own stories.

"They're sneaky!" snapped Mal.

"They can't be trusted!" grumbled Marion.

Shirley added, "The insurance companies are the worst. They keep paying out, but they don't care. They know they will get all the money they need from their premiums. They're allowed to take funds that are expected to be paid to a premium holder and put them aside to collect interest and be tax deductible."

Erin's voice boomed out with, "I paid premiums for two medical insurances and expected to get paid from both. No! Oh, no! They said you are only allowed to get paid by one and recover only what you have to pay extra for from the other. Did the insurance rep tell me that? No! But, they both kept taking out the same amount of premiums. What kind of crap is that?"

Marion timidly raised her hand and said in a very meek, low voice, "Every time I go to my doctor, he doesn't want to see me. He has my prescriptions already made out, waiting right there for me. His body language in that chair behind that dumb desk is telling me, 'Here are your pills, beat it!'"

Mal spoke again, "I get so discouraged with my doctor. I just don't want to see him. But who else can I go to? I'm stuck!"

Shirley came up with, "Hold on! Let me tell you this one! I lost six months of Social Security benefits because I didn't know they were available. I had been paying for twenty years and never received any information regarding the benefits available to me. It seems the only way you can find out is when you become disabled. Then it's up to a friend of a friend to let you know about the benefits!"

"Didn't the hospital's Social Service notify you of the benefits?" Kay asked.

Shirley answered, "The only time the Social Service of a hospital will show any concern for a patient is when he is unable to pay his bill. Then he gets all the attention!"

"Right on!" someone retorted.

Suddenly, our attention was captured by Archie, who had been very silent during the rapping. Archie nearly screamed, "I AM SO ANGRY!" His voice shook, and his chin trembled as he went on, "YEAH, I'M ANGRY! THEY WON'T PAY ME MY WORKMAN'S COMPENSATION!"

Archie's tone of voice and his entire body became rigid. You could see all the anger that he had been holding in. He couldn't let it go. I wondered if he was going to erupt. The more he talked, the angrier his tone and body became.

Archie reminded me of Claudia and the blanket.

Archie spit out, "THEY KEEP TELLING ME THAT I'M OKAY, and I can go back to work. If that's so, what then am I doing here?"

His whole body seemed to turn beet red. The skin that was visible certainly was. Every vein looked like a rope under his skin. He was just like Claudia.

Kay quickly left the room. Watching her leave, I started to follow. Agnes noticed my intentions and motioned with her hand for me to remain seated. Resettling into my chair, it seemed that this man was raging on and I didn't want to stay there. I was very uncomfortable. It seemed like only a second had elapsed before Kay returned clutching two pillows.

What was Kay going to do with two pillows, I wondered. This was no time to lie down. My anxiety started to grow.

Kay motioned to a patient sitting on the couch. She wanted him to get up. The pillows were placed in the vacated spot of the couch. Archie kept ranting and raging, repeating over and over again, "They won't pay me my Workman's Compensation!" He headed for the couch. His voice never stopped agonizing over his situation. Archie seemed to know what he was doing. He knelt down in front of the pillows and began vigorously beating them. He was beating the hell out of them. My imagination began to work overtime. I imagined the pillows to be a face and saw torrents of blood pouring out of them. Then Agnes began groaning and crying, as if he was actually beating her instead of the pillow. Archie began hitting harder.

Other patients began moaning and groaning. Kay was saying, "Please don't, you're hurting me!" Mal cried, "Don't hit me any more. I'll give you your money. Please don't hit me! Please!"

It continued. Sweat was pouring from my body. Agnes came over to me, smiling. Nothing seemed to be bothering her. She placed her hand on my shoulder, comforting me.

I noticed that Callie and Alex, who hadn't said a word, seemed to feel the same way I had when Claudia was under the blanket. They looked as surprised as I had felt then.

The punching Archie began to ease up on the pillows and finally stopped. He was completely exhausted. Sliding to the floor, he went limp. His whole body was at rest, soaked with sweat. Kay sat next to him and began wiping the perspiration from his face. Amazingly, Archie seemed to show a peacefulness. Serenity washed over his face that hadn't been there before. It was relaxed. He began to look unburdened, just like Claudia had after the blanket act.

"How do you feel?" Kay asked Archie.

There was a long pause as Archie caught his breath. He had slumped onto the floor "I feel like a new man. I feel better than ever before. Did I ever get all of that out of me! Am I glad it's all gone."

Agnes spoke directing her words at Callie and Alex. She explained to them that they had witnessed a structure and repeated the same definition that Charley had given to me. She turned to me saying, "Ed, you just saw another structure that can be used for releasing anger. You have seen the blanket, the pool, and now the pillow. There are many more that can be used and you will see them all.

Agnes went on to explain that having someone accompany you through the structure was another way to enhance the release of the anger. It's known as "accommodating." If someone is there with you, the ordeal becomes more realistic, and the anger is fully dealt with.

Alex asked the question I asked Charley after Claudia's blanket episode. "Suppose you get angry outside and begin to beat up on someone. You could inflict injury on that person. That could be dangerous."

Archie snapped, "Wait a minute ..." Archie, a burly man who had a loud, brusque voice which now sounded tired, was back in his chair. He spoke very slowly. "You asked if it was possible to inflict injury on someone if you dealt with anger the way I did. I know when I'm angry, and I know when I'm hurt. I'm aware of the differences. When the anger is there, I'm not going to be carrying pillows around. Only when I get to a safe place will I deal with it, like at home in my bedroom. I'm certainly not going to advertise it everywhere. I'd be locked up if I did. But, I'm in complete control. Therefore, I can deal with it correctly. It looks hairy and scary, but the feeling while I'm dealing with it is rewarding."

Archie leaned forward in his chair and continued, "When you do get rid of the anger in this fashion, you must make certain that you get it all out. You'll know when that has happened. You'll become completely exhausted. The exhaustion will force your body to become relaxed. That's what you're looking for, the relaxed part. If you don't feel relaxed you haven't dealt with your anger. You're holding in something, and the experience will not have been fulfilling." Archie sighed and leaned back in his chair.

Smiling, Agnes interrupted, "We have to stop now. Our time is up."

I got up, looked at Mal slyly, and said, "I always thought pillows were for your head to sleep on."

21

TORPEDO BACKSCULLING

Lena's massages were certainly a highlight of the Pain Unit. Her massages transported a tense body into a relaxed state of being. That state was reinforced by my next activity, the pool, and its ninety-six degree heat. If I could, I'd stay in that pool all day.

When I arrived at the pool, I saw an elderly person doing a strange thing. He wasn't swimming. He was floating, but not in a way that was familiar to me. I had never seen anything like it. He was floating on his back and moving forward, FEET FIRST. He reached the other side of the pool, pushed off with his feet, and began backstroking toward the opposite end. His arms did not come out of the water as in a normal backstroke. Instead, they went up along the side of his body. When they were above his head, he kept them outstretched and quickly brought them down to the side of his body. You could see the powerful propulsion he created to drive himself backwards. When he reached the opposite side, his hands were outstretched above his head. He pushed off, somehow propelling himself so that he was moving, FEET FIRST, to the opposite side. He looked like a torpedo in the water. How did he do that?

Each patient who arrived saw the strange sight and was also amazed. Everyone cautiously gathered to one side in the pool without disturbing him. A patient who had to use a walker was slow in arriving and held up our activity. With difficulty, he managed to get in and hugged our side of the pool as he joined us. Then Cheryl called out for our attention.

While the floater continued his laps, Cheryl spoke, "Today, we have a graduate from the Pain Unit who is demonstrating his new way of floating. He has been experimenting with it for a long time. It's called, "Torpedo Back Sculling." His name is Mr. John Fisher."

I listened to her, watched him closely and tried to figure out how he was doing that float. Somehow, he was propelling himself with his hands above his head. I couldn't make it out.

Cheryl continued, "He came to the Pain Unit with intractable pain caused by his lamanectomies. The good news is he has now resumed a normal fruitful life. He attributes it to the skills the Pain Unit taught him, and especially, the floating you are now watching him do. Mr. Fisher will now explain his Torpedo Back Sculling, and how it came about."

She beckoned to him. He sculled to where we were standing, stopped, set his feet down, and greeted us. We welcomed him warmly. Our words echoed throughout the room. Mr. Fisher was friendly and enthusiastic, as he spoke of his unique way of swimming. "I learned how to do the float at the University's pool. I had become acquainted with a lifeguard who taught me how to do the Australian crawl. She was also a member of the school's water ballet group.

"One day, while I was practicing my crawl, she was doing the Torpedo Back Sculling. There she was coming towards me, feet first. I couldn't believe what I was seeing. I stopped in my lane and watched this strange swim. I was curious so I interrupted her swim concentration when she came back to her starting point. She didn't mind the interruption and explained the stroke to me. She told me that during her water ballet performances, while opening and closing the 'flower', the performers closed it with the torpedo back sculling. That's what she was practicing now. I asked her if she would teach it to me, and she cheerfully agreed."

A patient interrupted, "You must have the right body with enough buoyancy to be able to float like that. Isn't that correct?"

"Yes, you must be buoyant," Mr. Fisher answered. "You must also understand where that buoyancy comes from. It comes from your body being completely relaxed. If your body is tense, you lose that buoyancy. You will tend to sink and must scull to stay afloat. The massages, physical therapy, breathing exercises, ability to deal with my anger, and all the other skills I've learned here at the Pain Unit had rid my body of tension, leaving it completely relaxed. Whenever a tension spot settled into my body, I knew it was there and relieved it with my breathing. I also learned to use breathing in rhythm with my floating. The lifeguard taught me how to do that."

He demonstrated the breathing technique by placing his arms out along the coping of the pool wall and letting his body float in the water. He took a deep breath, held it for a moment, and exhaled. His body rose when he inhaled and held it. It sank when he exhaled. The rising and sinking motions were subtle, but they could be seen.

"Did you notice my body rise on the inhale and sink on the exhale?" Mr. Fisher asked.

Some of the patients nodded and some didn't.

Mr. Fisher continued, "Now, I will float, take deep breaths and exhale. Watch what happens to my body?"

I watched. His body seemed to be in rhythm with his breathing. Whenever he exhaled his legs began to sink. As soon as he inhaled, his legs rose to the surface of the water. He didn't have to scull at all to stay afloat. He just lay there in the water. I remembered a newspaper photo of a person floating on the Dead Sea, reading a newspaper. Mr. Fisher reminded me of that photo. The only difference was the Dead Sea was all salt, and a person could easily float in it. The pool has no salt. Maybe Mr. Fisher was right. The body had to be relaxed. Mr. Fisher was definitely relaxed. I knew it and could see it.

Archie asked sarcastically, "What good does that float do you?"

Mr. Fisher explained, "When you float with your arms outstretched above your head, you have aligned your spine with the center of gravity. This alignment is free from the differential pull of gravity. When you're sculling in that position, you are doing a marvelous stretching exercise. Your posture will automatically begin to correct itself. It's far superior to the traction gear hospitals use to align your back. Not only that, but your blood flows freely, parallel with gravity, instead of going up and down. Nothing in your body is bent to block its flow. I can actually feel my blood flowing. Every time I do it, I feel better than ever."

Archie was still doubting and belligerent. He said, "Why can't I just lie on the floor and imitate the floating?"

Mr. Fisher answered, "By lying on the floor, the spine isn't free to settle into its proper alignment. Anything that is supporting the back is not allowing the spine to align itself in its free state, like water does. In water, you eliminate all pressure points that would occur from lying down on the floor or bed. Water, in itself, is therapeutic. We were born out of a pool of water."

I asked Mr. Fisher, "How do you propel yourself during that float?"

Mr. Fisher took his hands out of the water and said, "When you scull, both your hands are moving in a half circle pushing the water behind you. The speed and force you use to push the water will determine the speed with which you will be propelled. When doing this, I'll do one lap using both hands at the same time. I alternate hands during the next lap, using one and then the other. Using the two types of sculling allows me to keep track of how many laps I've done."

A silence descended. Cheryl asked, "Does anyone have anymore questions for Mr. Fisher?" The silence continued.

Cheryl added to Mr. Fisher's explanation, "Swimming is excellent posture therapy. If you float on your back, with arms stretched out above the head, your posture will then automatically correct itself."

Cheryl looked at Mr. Fisher and said, "John, we thank you for your demonstration of Torpedo Back Sculling." She looked at the group and said, "Those who want to learn it can come to the pool every Wednesday night. Mr. Fisher will be here to teach you how to do it. Thank you again, Mr. Fisher."

Everyone clapped. Mr. Fisher acknowledged the accolade, climbed out of the pool, grabbed his towel, and left.

We had a few more minutes to stay in the pool so Cheryl threw in the ball. The ball was usually the first part of the pool activity, but today it turned out to be the last. We fought to keep it above the water. It was fun getting to the ball and striking it to keep it from landing on the water. I was amazed at how agile I was becoming in the water. Still, while my back didn't hurt while I was hitting the ball, it always hurt after I got out of the pool.

The patient who had been late amazed me. He was going after that ball like a ten-year-old. He would jump as if he weren't disabled. How could he do that? During one of his jumps, he seemed to realize what he was doing, immediately stopped and began limping out of the pool.

Cheryl called, "Time is up everybody. Everyone out of the pool"

As I was getting out of the pool, one thought was on my mind. How did you know when your body was relaxed?

22

I HATE MY BODY

"Ed!"

I tried to keep my eyes on the floor, but his voice came across the room demanding a response. I looked up.

Charley spoke again, "How about you, Ed? Would you like to take the next turn?"

My eyes then fixed on his red beard, hoping someone else would interrupt and take the turn. No one did. Why did he choose me? I had to take my turn because I didn't know how to say no. I never knew how to say no. I also didn't want anyone to think that I was scared, or had anything to hide. Still, my mind always filled with suspicion about some ulterior motive which must be behind all this talk. Getting me to beat the pillow or scream into it. Yeah, that's what he wants me to do. I don't want to do that, but I didn't have the guts to tell him.

"Okay, Charley, I'll go next," I said. "But, I don't want to beat any pillows or get under a blanket. I don't like that. That's not for me."

I was shocked at what I was saying. I was never assertive like that. What had gotten into me? I wanted to run and catch those words and swallow them before they reached him.

Charley responded, "Ed, you only do what you want to do. You're not being forced into something you don't want to do. Remember, you call the shots. You quit when you want to quit."

"I want to believe you," I answered. "It's just that ... well ..."

"What is it, Ed?"

"Well, sometimes ... I'm scared. I think you're hypnotizing me." It came out. I finally found the courage to say out loud what I had been thinking for a long time.

Charley changed his position in the chair and a hand went up to his beard, "Ed, you're not. Believe me, you're not being hypnotized."

That was all he needed to say. His words were full of compassion and empathy. Something about the tone of his voice and his body and everything else about him seemed to assure me that I wasn't being hypnotized. I was convinced. A warm comforting feeling flooded over me when he said it. His whole essence told me that I was wrong. I felt guilty for having suggested it.

"Charley, I'm sorry. I'm sorry I mistrusted you. I believe you now." My voice broke. I had to clear my throat.

"Thank you, Ed. Now, let's continue with your turn."

My mind began searching for something to talk about. I finally said, "I'm more comfortable now, but I just don't know where to start."

Charley asked, "Do you remember the last session, Ed, when you blurted out that you hated your body?"

"Oh yes, I sure do. I can't understand why anyone would like a body wracked with so much pain."

"Good, then let's start with that, Ed. Why do you hate your body?"

"Why? Why do I hate my body? I just gave you a good reason. I'm in pain. If that isn't enough, here's more." My voice started to rise in pitch and volume. I was hollering, hoping that the loudness would drive home my point.

"What good has it been to me? All it wants is operations. It seems the only comfortable place for this body is in hospitals getting cut up, waited on, getting spoiled, and getting fixed on drugs."

I moved back and forth in my chair changing positions, my voice rigid with anger. "Everything is done for me in hospitals. Sometimes I think this body only wants attention. It's already marked with scars from eleven operations. It took thirteen months in hospitals to get them. That's why I hate my body."

I quickly raised my right pant leg and revealed a scar on the inside of my knee and roared, "Here's one of the scars. Do you want to see more?"

Charley's gaze never wavered. He sat perfectly still in his chair. I carried on as though someone had turned an electric switch on to start my motor moving. I let it all out. "This body is fat. It has colitis. It's addicted to smoking. It's addicted to booze and drugs. My wife doesn't go chasing after it either. I'm asking you? Would you like to have a body like mine, all fat, scarred, and addicted?"

I looked at the circle of patients and bellowed, "How about the rest of you? Would you like it?"

No one answered. They all looked like zombies sitting there in their chairs. I could see Mal rubbing her arms and fidgeting in her chair. The pain in her arms must have been intolerable.

I didn't want to stop. I was on a roll. Nothing could stop me now. I dredged up bitter memories of years of hate as I continued, "All this body has ever given me is pain. LOTS OF IT! It still does. The only peace I get from it is when I can get some sleep. Even then, my dreams are wrought with the ugliness of it. This body has even contemplated suicide. I HATE MY BODY!"

Mal got up, rubbing one arm then the other. She began pacing and continued her rubbing. I could see Charley's eyes scrutinizing her while I continued. "Yes! I do hate it. I know it's the only one I've got, but it has given me too many problems. What can I do? I can't work; I can't even play with my children. All I can do is lie in bed and watch my wife go to work."

Mal returned to her chair, rubbing her arms more vigorously. Charley whispered something to Agnes and Kay. They both got up and left.

"What part of your body would you like to change, Ed?" Charley asked with great calm in his voice.

How could he be so calm while I was bellowing at everyone?

"I would like to change ..." I drooped my head to look at my body, then raised it. My tirade was ebbing. I was feeling wrung out. I was limp. Charley's quiet manner was calming me. "I would like to change ..." Again, I drooped my head to see what part to change. Again, I raised my head and in a much softer voice, almost a whisper, I said, "I don't know right now. I guess the whole body, but I'm not certain."

Agnes and Kay returned with a screen divider and placed it in front of Mal. My eyes traveled across the room and watched it come to rest in front of Mal. It struck me as very strange. I was dumbfounded. I couldn't see Mal. Why had Agnes and Kay done that?

Charley repeated, "Ed, I asked what part of your body would you like to change? Tell me which part?"

I tried to pull my thoughts together. I wanted to answer Charley. "Something is happening to me, Charley. Something I don't understand. I don't know what's going on. My mind has gone blank. I've never hollered at anyone like that before. I'm sorry ... I'm sorry about everything, I'm sorry I'm alive. I can't think of what part I would like to change. I don't think ... I really want to change any part of my body," I said, with great difficulty.

"Charley, I don't know what's wrong. The blood is rushing to my head. I feel very anxious. I feel as if I am angry with myself for what I said. I'm having trouble thinking. A strange feeling is developing inside me. I don't know if it's anger, sadness, hopelessness or what. I don't know what to do with this feeling."

"You're doing fine, Ed." Charley reassured. "Don't hold onto it. Just let it keep coming out."

I believed him. I had no trouble believing him.

"There seems to be a lot of energy that's being generated inside. I don't really like what I said about my body. It's not true. My body is okay. There's nothing wrong with it." My voice became strong once again and I bellowed, "MY BODY IS OKAY!

"DO YOU HEAR! My body is okay."

Tears began flowing down my cheeks. I got off my chair and began pacing. I turned toward Charley and shouted, "THERE IS NOTHING WRONG WITH MY BODY!"

I paused and looked toward the screen divider, then toward Charley again and said, "I can feel something very strong welling up inside of me." I turned furiously to the group, swiveled my head around to look back at Charley, and tried to look at Mal. "WHAT IS HAPPENING TO ME?" I demanded an answer.

Again Charley whispered to Agnes. She nearly ran to the room entrance and picked up the two pillows that were lying on top of the mattresses. Just as quickly as she left, she returned clutching the two pillows.

I was breathing very heavily. I stared at the pillows she was holding. Grace motioned to the patient on the couch to move. The pillows were placed one on top of the other in the vacated spot.

"Try it, Ed," Charley insisted. "Try it!"

I knew then that I was angry—very angry. I looked at those pillows and knew what I had to do. Going over to the pillows, I knelt down and stared hard at them. Then I raised my arms and hit them. I heard, "Oh...that hurt Ed."

I hit them again. Again, I heard, "OH ... Ed. You're hurting me."

I began hitting harder. Kay began groaning and crying, as if I were actually beating her instead of the pillows. Other patients joined in to accommodate. One was saying, "Please don't. You're hurting me!" Another said, "Don't hit me any more. Please don't hit me! Please!" The more moans and groans I heard, the harder I hit the pillows. I could feel all the energy built up inside of me being transferred to the pillows. I was beating the hell out of them, beating, beating, beating—the moanings and groanings kept urging me on.

"You're doing fine, Ed." I couldn't make out who'd said it. "Get that anger out! Get every bit of it out, Ed. Don't hold it in."

My arms were tiring. They felt like lead pipes. I couldn't raise them anymore. The energy I had at the beginning was subsiding. Finally, my arms and head fell onto the pillows and I let them lie there. My upper body just sank into the couch. My hips slumped onto the floor.

Charley came up to me, put his hand on my shoulder, and asked, "Ed, are you all right?"

Breathing heavily and exhausted, I turned my head to look at this wonderful man and sighed, "Yes, I'm all right. I feel done in." Dazed, I didn't know what to say or do. I looked around at the group and back at Charley. My voice was coming back. I could speak. "I guess I'm tired. Strange, though, how good I feel. I don't feel any pain in my back or arms or anywhere. Why do I feel so relaxed?"

Charley sat next to me on the couch and began explaining slowly and carefully, "Ed, you did a worthwhile structure. You've just released a great deal of negative energy.

"That was your suppressed anger. I believe now you know there is a lot of anger pent up inside of you. This anger is probably what is causing most of your pain. You did say you felt no pain, and I can see how relaxed you are at this moment. Unfortunately, the pain will come back again and grasp you quickly. At least then you will know what anger really is. Do you feel good about the structure you've just done?"

I looked right at Charley, then turned to the others and said, "I can't put into words how I feel. It's just so amazing. It's the feeling after the anger was dealt with that's amazing. "Something was accomplished that I can't explain. Can I do it again?"

"No, Ed, not now. That was enough for you today," Charley smiled knowingly. "But, you will have the opportunity again. I have no doubts about that."

Grace and Kay removed the screen from in front of Mal.

"Charley, why was the screen placed in front of Mal? I know she was hurting, but she wasn't distracting me."

"I'm not sure, Ed, except that it was certain that she was getting painful vibrations from you. I used the screen to block those vibrations. It happens frequently that someone can relate to another's feelings, creating more pain within themselves. Did the screen help, Mal?"

"Yes, Charley, it did," Mal answered. "Your right! I was getting some kind of vibes from Ed. The more he spoke about hating his body, the more I hurt. When he shouted that he hated his body and contemplated suicide, I received jolts of pain. I was ready to leave the room. When the screen shut off the sight of Ed, the pain subsided. What an experience! Let's keep that screen nearby."

"Okay," Charley said. "Your time is up, Ed."

I rose from the floor with little if any difficulty—light as a feather. I knew I was walking, but I felt nothing underneath me.

Charley asked, "Who wants to be next?"

23

SEX LANGUAGE

I was gazing out the window, studying the slope where skiers enjoyed their runs. The ski run was under high-tension wires, and the sun cast straight-lined shadows onto the slope. They intrigued my senses. There was something about straight lines that impressed me. It was near noontime, and the line shadows seemed to ski up and down the slope. I couldn't understand my senses acting this way.

"Hey, Ed," came a voice from behind. It was Ernie. His tone was flat—probably from drying out. He walked towards me, stopped at the window, and looked out. He was only half my size and didn't take up much of the window. Ernie didn't say much. Most of the time people didn't realize he was in their company. He was here as an alcoholic.

"What are you looking at, Ed?" Ernie said in a monotone.

"It's that ski slope over there," I answered. "There's something about the line shadows created by the sun and high-tension wires that has excited my feelings. Worse, I don't know if I should feel good or bad."

"Are you all right, Ed? You sound very strange."

"Yeah, I know," I answered, and thought for a moment. "You know what Ernie?"

"No! I don't know."

"I know now what this strange feeling is. When I arrived at the Pain Unit, I saw that slope. I thought about how I would like to climb it, and I never thought of it again until now. ERNIE, I'M GOING TO CLIMB THAT HILL!"

"Ed, you're nuts." Ernie meant it.

"I'm going to climb that son-of-a-gun. That's why the strange feeling came over me. I want to climb that hill."

Ernie pushed me aside and said, "Let me get a better look at that slope." He looked. "It's not too difficult a slope. You shouldn't have any problem with it. There is a trail leading up to the top." He thought for a moment, then faced me and said, "I'M GOING TO DO IT WITH YOU!"

"You want to do it with me?" I asked, totally surprised.

"Yes, I do."

"Okay, Ernie. We'll both climb it." Amazed that he would want to climb it with me, I asked, "When shall we do it?"

"Let's do it tomorrow."

"Yeah, we could do it right after Sensory Awareness. We're supposed to go outdoors for some kind of awareness deal. After it's over, we would have plenty of time to climb it before supper."

Ernie agreed and said, "We must make sure the staff is aware of what we want to do. I'll see to that."

We shook hands and agreed that it would be an accomplishment for both of us.

While shaking hands, we heard someone hollering outside my room. Startled, we went to the doorway. The loud voices were coming from the staff desk. Callie was there, with her hand shaking, and pointing a finger at a staff member we couldn't see.

She was screaming, "I can leave here anytime I want! No one can stop me! Do you hear?"

She was standing in front of the desk. A bag was on the floor next to her. She picked it up and headed our way, toward the stairs. As she was passing us she said, "I'm getting out of here! This place hasn't done anything for me. You'd be wise to get out too!"

Our eyes followed her through the hall as she disappeared down the stairs. I looked at Ernie and said, "She's leaving without her stretcher. How come?"

Ernie shrugged his shoulders and said, "I guess she has no need for it now. Okay Ed, I have to go now and get ready for a stupid rap session. See you tomorrow for the climb." He left.

I began to get ready for my psychomotor session. I checked my pack of cigarettes. It was pretty full, but I didn't want to take any chances of running out. I took another pack with me just in case and left. God, I wish I could quit.

When I entered the room, Mal and Marion were sitting in chairs that formed a part of the circle.

"Did you hear about Callie?" I asked as I entered.

"Yes."

"Boy, was she angry! She walked out of here without a stretcher. I wonder what happened to her."

Mal spoke, "She was told this morning that the stretcher wasn't available to her anymore. She would have to walk with a walker, or with an aide helping her. She refused, got very angry, and swore at the nurse. She got up out of her bed, got dressed, walked to the desk, and argued with the staff. Then she walked out of the rehab. I guess the staff felt if she could walk to the bathroom, then she could walk to the activities. Callie didn't see it that way and left."

I shook my head with amazement, took a seat next to Mal and Marion, and asked, "How are you today?"

Mal started to say, "I feel ..." but Marion interrupted with, "I'm terrible. I didn't get any sleep last night. My whole body feels like it exploded with pain all over."

I looked at Mal. Mal shrugged at me. At the same time Archie walked in. He was angry. Looking at us, he asked, "You know what just happened to me?"

The three of us shook our heads with a soft, "No."

"I have colitis, and sometimes there's blood on my stool. Whenever that happens, I'm supposed to inform the doctor. I did just that. I buzzed the desk because there was blood on my stool. Marty came into my room and asked what was wrong. I told her that there was blood on my stool, and before I flushed, she should check it out. She said, 'What! You want me to check your stool? Are you crazy? I'm not going to do that!' and walked out. What do I do now?"

Mal spoke, "Archie, don't tell Marty. Tell the doctor. Marty will always do that. She's not your doctor."

While Mal was advising Archie, Kay, Alice, and Charley entered the room. They were followed by the rest of the group. Our greetings were reciprocated, and we all settled into the circle of seats.

A few moments later Charley said, "We're all here. Let's begin. Who wants to start?"

I thought of the talk I'd had with Lena about my constellation and about not being able to stop Agnes. I said, "I'll start."

"Good, Ed. You can begin any time," Charley said, settling back comfortably in his chair.

I was feeling more comfortable with these sessions and was almost willing to discuss anything that was bothering me. I took a deep breath and whined, "Charley, what does all this mean, my constellation, not being able to stop Alice from barreling over me, and this circle bit? What's a 'limit'? To me a limit is what I can do and what I can't do. Lena did try to explain them, but to no avail. All this is too deep for me. I need answers that I can understand and deal with."

Charley paused for a few seconds, and said, "Yes, Ed. You do deserve an explanation for those structures. I hope I can satisfy you with my answers."

Charley's voice was soothing. I felt comfortable with the way he was talking. His body language, with an accent on the tone of his words, was hypnotic and therapeutic. I began to see him as a role model.

Charley continued, "Ed, your constellation has five brothers, the sixth child, a sister, the seventh, you, and the eighth, another sister. Being born between two sisters, after five brothers, created deficiencies in your upbringing. Mainly, love and attention were minimal for you. Your growth in that kind of an environment had mixed blessings. Love and attention came to you at the price of some kind of illness, like your operations.

"Not being able to stop Agnes reinforced the lack of love and attention. Agnes represented that love and attention you were demanding, in any form, that you didn't get as a child. You wanted her to bowl you over. Now, remember all of this is due to your subconscious working very hard to satisfy your needs.

"The circle represented your limits and boundaries. You were in and out of the circle—no limits—no boundaries. Your operations were connected to what you called 'hot spots' that you were in. You were externalizing. You mentioned how you were ill prepared for college. You accepted advice from others who said you had enough preparation to enter. Yet, you admitted being ill prepared. Again, you're externalizing. You knew you weren't prepared for college, but went anyway.

"Your sick brother got all the attention; your subconscious learned from him how to get attention. It was the only way you knew how to get it. It boils down to getting attention from outside of Ed."

"Wait a minute!" I interrupted. "What does this outside and externalizing mean?"

Charley answered, "It means you became more concerned about what happened outside of you than inside of you. You never learned to heed your own feelings. Instead, you learned from others how to get the attention you needed. You have been programmed by family, by school, and by religion to know what you know, to feel what you feel, to think what you think, and to see what you see. You've been taught nothing about boundaries and limits. Unfortunately,

most of us have that same problem. If you had been taught
to form boundaries, you would have known your limits and
would have made more effective decisions. You would have
known how to think and feel from the inside and then could
have related to the outside world. You would have relied on
your own decisions, rather than on what someone else had
suggested. You would know your limits." Charley paused,
looked straight into my eyes and said, "Can you grasp some
of this, Ed?"

"I don't know, Charley," I said, feeling deflated and
downhearted. "That sounds like a whole new world I must
learn to live in."

"Yes," Charley replied. "It will be a whole new world for
you and a very productive one. I'll guarantee that. You
have the opportunity, here at the Pain Unit, to enter that new
world. I have noticed some positive signs coming from you.
I know, you'll make it."

"I hear what you're saying, Charley," I said. "Every bit
of it is new to me. I sense that all my decisions are
influenced by other people. You're right. I don't know how
to allow my feelings to influence my decisions. I never
learned how. I'm ready to learn."

"That's what I want to hear, Ed. Now let us go on."

I waited a moment for his next move.

Charley asked, "Ed, are you satisfied with your sex life?"

My face automatically flushed. I couldn't speak. I
searched my brain, hoping to find some way to deflect the
question. Instead, it signaled my heart to beat faster, heating
up my body, sending out a cold sweat, and finally settling
onto my face, reddening like a cooked lobster. "Should I
answer him with the truth--or a lie?" I thought. If I lied,
more blood would deepen the red in my face, and the sweat
would pour out of me.

"Yes, I am," I said hoarsely. In defense I continued, "I
don't know what it means to be sexually satisfied."

"You don't know what I mean?" Charley asked.

"Well, not really. I would never be comfortable having sex with anyone except my wife. She's the only one. I have no other experience. How would I know?"

I could feel his eyes penetrating right to my core; yet, it wasn't a stinging penetration. As usual, there was compassion in his eyes and his voice. They gave me the comfort I needed to tell the truth. I couldn't lie to him. Suddenly, I couldn't say anything. I began to tighten up and felt myself being tied into a straight jacket, fighting it all the way.

"NO!" I said it emphatically. "I'm not sexually satisfied! I'm not." I began crying. Someone handed me a tissue, which I took and used to wipe away my tears.

"Ed, do you and your wife have a sex language?"

As he spoke, I could feel his sympathy. He had the ability to make it easy to tell him anything he wanted to know.

"A sex language? We don't talk dirty to one another," I answered. That drew coarse laughs from the others. Their laughter bewildered me.

Charley explained, "I don't mean talking dirty. When you are in need of sex, how do you communicate that need to her? Do you have any special words or phrases to act as hints for sex? Do you use any sexually explicit words?"

"No, I don't," I stuttered.

"Does your wife?"

"No, she doesn't."

"Then you don't really have any sex language to communicate your desire to have sex?"

Sheepishly, I answered, "I guess I don't. We use the rhythm system, because we don't want many children. We wait five days before and five days after her period. Then we allow it to happen. I don't ask for it. I wait and hope it happens. Charley, I can't get comfortable talking about this subject. I want to stop it."

"Ed, that is your feeling, and I will stop."   Charley understood. "You did very well."

Charley sat back in his chair, closed his eyes for a moment, and said, "Who wants to be next?"

I settled into my chair and thought, now I have to learn a sex language. How do I do that?

24

AWARENESS

On my way to the gym-room I caught up with Ernie and asked, "Hey, Ernie! Did you notify the desk of our plan to climb the ski slope today?"

"Hi, Ed," he said in his usual monotone. "Yes, I told them at the desk of our planned venture. I had to sign out, and before we leave, you'll have to sign out, too. They wouldn't let me do it for you."

"Good, that's no problem. I can do it." I wondered if he noticed how happy I felt.

"Cheryl was at the desk too," he said. "She heard me mention our venture and thought it a great idea. She said to see her when our awareness thing is over. She has some suggestions for us."

I asked, "I wonder what they are?"

We entered the gym-room and greeted those already there. They echoed our greetings, while lying on matted tables and on top of floor mats.

Ernie chose a floor mat. I chose a tablemat because it would be easier for me to get up. It wasn't too long before the rest of the group arrived and took their places.

We were all present.

Cheryl greeted us and said, "Let's get into a comfortable position. Make sure there is nothing on your person to create any discomforts while doing the exercise."

I took off my shoes, unbuckled my belt, took my wallet out of my back pocket, and put it next to my head. I was ready.

Cheryl waited until we were all ready.

She started, "I know, at times, it's very difficult to stay awake during this period. But it's very important to remain awake in order to be aware. Falling asleep will not give you the full benefit of awareness while you relax. This relaxing exercise has a two-fold purpose: to sharpen your awareness and to let you know when you are relaxed. A sharp awareness will show where the tension spots in your body have rooted. Then, the tension can be relieved by this relaxing exercise and other learned relaxation techniques. Let's try to work on our awareness and relaxation, and not fall asleep. Another very important point is to try and visualize all the areas I mention. For instance, when I say take a deep breath, visualize the breath as a ball of air entering your mouth. When I say lips, visualize the ball of air moving over your lips. When I say lungs, visualize your lungs like an elongated balloon expanding from the ball of air entering them. Be creative with your visualization."

Cheryl paused to allow what she'd said to sink in.

"Take a deep breath," Cheryl continued. "Concentrate on the air passing over your lips. Feel how cool it is goes down your throat, expanding your lungs, and stomach. Hold it for a moment. Now, let it out, very slowly. Very slowly let the air come out. Be aware of the air, now passing over your lips, being warm. Your lungs are contracting, along with your stomach. Be aware of what's happening to the rest of your body.

"Take another deep breath. This time create an image in your mind of the cool air passing over your lips, how it is expanding your lungs, and stomach. Again, hold it there for a moment, and form a vivid image of what is actually happening inside of you.

"Take another deep breath. Allow this breath to sharpen your awareness, through images about what it is doing inside of you."

Cheryl paused, then continued. "Think of the top your head. Get a good image of it. Visualize the hair covering the scalp. Tighten that scalp. Tighten it as tight as you can.

Picture the scalp as tight as a drum and the hair standing up straight. Hold it there for a couple of seconds."

I couldn't tell if I was tightening my head or my brow. Whatever was tightening became uncomfortable.

"Now, slowly, very slowly, relax it. Notice how comfortable it is as you're relaxing the tightness. Now, release the tightening. Allow the scalp to relax. Let it relax completely. Don't allow a single tight spot to remain. It is completely relaxed, and you can feel all the tightness has left. The top of your head feels so good. It is now completely relaxed.

"Think of the top of your head, and how nice and relaxed it feels."

I did notice that the top my head, or brow, felt good. There was a marked difference between the top of my head and the area below it.

Cheryl went on, "Think of your forehead. Tighten it. Tighten it as much as you can, so tight that you're beginning to get a headache. You can't tighten anymore. You can't stand it. Hold it there. Think of how uncomfortable your forehead feels being so tight. You want to release it. Not yet. Now, release it. Let the tightness slowly go away. It is starting to relax. You can feel your forehead beginning to relax as you slowly release the tightness. It is almost completely relaxed. You can't wait until it is all relaxed. Release all the tightness. Let it all go. Now your forehead is completely relaxed. It is completely and totally relaxed. Your forehead feels so good. It is completely relaxed.

"Think of the top of your head, and how nice and relaxed it feels.

"Think of your forehead, and how nice and relaxed it feels."

Cheryl took us through the eyes, nose, mouth, and chin. I couldn't believe the difference between my head and the rest of my body. My head felt detached from my body, as if it were floating in the air. What a wonderful feeling!

Visualizing was difficult for me. I tried to form pictures of the parts of the body she mentioned. The pictures wouldn't form, but I could feel how relaxed those body parts were. After relaxing each body part, she went back to the top of the head and repeated the same phrases for each part, to be sure it was relaxed. That made the whole exercise really work.

Cheryl called up our shoulders, torso, legs, ankles, and feet. She ended with, "Your whole body is now completely and totally relaxed. Every part of you feels like it is floating. All the tensions are gone. There are no tight areas. You are completely free from all the tensions that have been built up through the years. You feel so good. You never realized that such a tension-free state was possible in your body. You are going to keep it there. You're never going to lose it. It just feels so good. Every day you are going to feel better and better. Yes, every day in every way, you're going to be better and better and better. And, that is so.

"Now, before you get up, open your eyes. Have them see what is in front of you. Let your eyes know where you are. Start to stretch. Start with your arms, your legs, and your body. Stretch all of them out. Have a big yawn and take in all the new oxygen that is going to make you feel great. Now you may get up. Get up slowly. Get your body acclimatized to your surroundings. There, you're all set and feeling fine."

I did as she said. I had the biggest yawn of all. The feeling in which my body had luxuriated was foreign to me. I had never felt like that before, except when I was massaged by Lena. Now I had learned how to get to that euphoric state without the aid of a massage. Why was all this so secret? This was the height of relaxation. It's needed for all back problems. It's better than any medication. I searched the faces of the others to see if they had benefited as well as I had. Some were disgruntled; others indifferent. I asked Mal how she felt. She said she loved it, but had trouble staying awake. I said I didn't know if I was awake or if I had slept.

I knew I'd heard every word Cheryl was saying. "It's funny, I can almost repeat her words verbatim. Her words have stayed with me."

Ernie and I approached Cheryl. She asked, "How did the exercise go for you?"

I said, "My body never felt better. I don't know if I slept through it, but I bet I can repeat every word you used to relax."

"Good!" Cheryl said. "How about you, Ernie?"

"I just can't keep awake during it. I try, but I always fall asleep," Ernie answered.

Cheryl turned to me and said, "Ed, I was there when Ernie informed the desk about the two of you climbing the ski slope. Think of this while you're walking up the slope. When you get there, eye the height, the path you'll take, and have a good image of it in your mind. Take two or three deep breaths, then start the walk slowly. Don't rush it, and only concentrate on where your legs are landing on the ground in front of you. Don't look up or down to see how far you've progressed. Do it for a distance, then stop. See how far you have gone and enjoy what you see. When you are ready, start again, following the same routine, and don't forget the deep breaths. Just keep concentrating on your legs and the ground they are walking on. You will then get to the top before you know it."

"How will that be of any help to us?" I asked.

Cheryl answered, "Each time you stop will be like a time for refueling your body, to keep going. The walking and concentrating will keep your mind and brain absorbed by your legs and the ground in front of you. They won't be distracted by any pain, by how much further you must go, or by how much longer it will take. You can do it."

"Thanks, Cheryl. I know I can do it."

Ernie meekly said, "We'd better get going."

Ernie and I headed for the slope. It was a very short distance. When we got there, I looked at Ernie and asked, "Are you ready?"

"Yeah, I guess so."

I did what Cheryl suggested. I eyed the path leading to the top and noticed brush and stones on either side. I bent my head low enough to see my legs and the ground they would cover. Taking two deep breaths, I started, keeping my eyes on the ground and concentrating on what my legs were doing. My legs moved and the ground passed under them. I concentrated wholly on that small area where I could see the movement, not lifting my head once. On and on I went, as the unfamiliar ground passed beneath me.

I stopped, took some deep breaths, and then looked around me. What a beautiful sight! I was only a short distance away from where I had started. I prepared for another jaunt, took some deep breaths, and followed the same routine. I don't know how many times I stopped, but each time the view was gorgeous and got better with each stop. I couldn't wait to get to the top, but knew better than to rush it, so I kept the same rhythm going. My body began to feel exhaustion, especially as the angle of ascent increased. Suddenly the ground leveled off, and I was on top of the slope.

I couldn't believe I had done it. I was on top of the slope, enjoying a magnificent view! There was the lake in back of the rehab adding beauty to the scene. Ernie was right behind me. I don't think he was as elated as I was.

"Ernie, we made it!" I grabbed him and hugged him. "We made it. Can you believe it?"

Ernie wasn't thrilled; he wasn't too happy.

"I've got to get in bed," he said and started down. I stayed a little longer to soak in every bit of the view. Then I started down.

Going down was easy, but I could see Ernie having trouble. Finally, we entered the Rehab and saw Marty. My first instinct was to tell her what we had accomplished.

I called to her, "Marty!"

She came over and asked, "What do you want?"

Happy as a lark, I said, "Ernie and I just climbed the ski slope. Isn't that great!"

"SO WHAT?" she retorted.

25

MAKE ME HAPPY

Charley got up, stretched, walked to the door, and returned. "Marion," he said, as he lowered himself into his chair, "we haven't heard from you in quite a spell. Will you take this turn?"

Marion became wide-eyed and was taken aback. She reluctantly answered, "Do I have to?"

"No, you don't," Charley said. "Like I said, it's been a very long time since you've taken a turn. How can we be of help if you don't?"

"All right, Charley, I'll take it," Marion said meekly.

"Good! Where do you want to start?"

Marion began fidgeting. She didn't want the turn, and unsettled in her chair, she replied, "I don't know why my husband can't make me happy. I try to make him happy all the time. What should I do?"

"Does he respond to your attempts to make him happy?" Charley asked.

Marion hesitated, and then said, "No! Not at all! No matter what I do, it doesn't make him happy."

"Marion, how do you make anyone happy?"

"By doing nice things. I do nice things for him. I cook, iron his clothes, and do the shopping; I even iron his socks. What else can I do?"

"Those are all external nice things." Charley asked, "Do you love your husband?"

"Yes!" Marion answered. "And, I love him very much. There isn't anyone else I love more."

"How does he know you love him very much?"

"I told you—all the nice things I do for him," Marion replied impatiently. "What else can I do?"

"Marion, let's do a structure."

"Oh, no. Oh ... I just don't want to do it," Marion muttered.

Charley ignored her response and said, "I would like you to choose a person in this group. Male or female. It doesn't matter. Pick someone now."

"Must I?" Marion whined.

"Yes, you must," Charley insisted.

Marion began nervously eyeing the group, her eyes jumping from one to the other, and said, "I don't know who to pick!"

"Anyone. Choose anyone."

Marion searched again and anxiously called out, "Kay! I want Kay."

"Good!" Turning, Charley smiled at Kay and asked, "Kay, will you accept?"

"Yes, Charley. I'd be glad to."

"Good! Kay would you please move your chair a couple of feet toward the center of the circle?"

Kay did as Charley asked and resumed her seat.

"Now, Marion, I want you to look at Kay and do whatever you can to make her happy."

Marion, confused, gaped at Charley. She was uneasy in her chair. She didn't know what to do.

Charley waited, but Marion didn't respond. He asked, "Marion did you hear what I asked?"

"I heard you, Charley!" Marion blurted loudly, "But, I can't think of anything that will make her happy. How can I make her happy?"

"By doing nice things," Charley replied. "Do some nice things that will make Kay happy."

"Charley ... I'm confused." Marion was trembling as she said, "I don't know what to do to make her happy. Why are you putting me through this?"

Avoiding Marion's anxiety, Charley continued, "Kay, make Marion happy."

Kay, slowly and clearly stated, "I can't. I can't make her happy, anymore than anyone else can."

"I know you can't, Kay." Charley agreed. Then he said, "Marion, did you hear what Kay said?"

"Yes," Marion said nervously. "Then how do you make someone happy?"

"Marion, you don't MAKE someone happy," Charley continued, with great tenderness and warmth. He leaned forward in his chair, his hands folded loosely in front of him. "You can't make anyone happy, or make them do anything. Instead, concentrate on making yourself happy, by changing your perception of happiness. Happiness comes from within you and from the heart. When you're happy, that happiness will radiate to your surroundings. Others will see that happiness as your aura and will react to it. When you, personally, are happy, that happiness is like a magnet. It will attract others to you like a magnet does metal."

Marion nervously said, "I don't know what you mean. I was brought up to make people happy."

Charley immediately interrupted, "Have you made any people happy?"

"No," Marion said softly and sadly. "No, I haven't."

Charley's body exuded sympathy. He lowered his voice almost to a whisper, extended his hand toward Marion, and repeated, "You can't control someone's senses or emotions, unless that person allows it. People are not robots. They are human beings who do what they want, provided they are free to do so. You can't make anyone happy. No one can. But the love that pours out of your heart, in the form of a 'being person' rather than a 'having person', will make people happy. You, too, like Ed, have been brought up to externalize, rather than to internalize. I suggest that you make yourself happy and let the world see it. Don't try to make anyone else happy."

"Charley, I disagree with you." Marion's anger was beginning to show. "I was brought up to make people happy, and that's what I'm going to do," she said emphatically. "I'm stopping this now!" She folded her arms, stiffened her body and meant it.

Charley didn't pursue it any further and ended the session.

I was puzzled by what had just happened. I was also brought up to make people happy. I saw the truth in what Charley had said. You cannot make anyone happy unless they give themselves to you, and will do as you say. I guessed that was another area I had to learn about. Make myself happy?

26

I HATE MOM

Another day, another session with Charley.

Charley settled his body in his chair and asked, "What's that on your arm, Ed?"

His voice caught me off guard. I had been talking with someone on the other side of me. I mumbled, "Oh, are you talking to me?"

"Yes! What's that on your arm?"

"It's a tattoo. I had it done while I was in the navy.

"What does the tattoo say?"

"I didn't want a tattoo with a girl's name on it. My brother had had one, and he'd married the girl. Now, they're divorced. It's very expensive to have tattoos removed. I figured I would be smarter than he was, so I had "MOM" put on."

"Have you ever thought of removing it?" Charley asked.

"What? No! That's my mother. I'd never think that." I felt offended. "Why do you ask?"

"You may want to." Charley spoke as if he meant what he said.

"Charley, I'll never want to," I replied and I meant it.

Charley sensed my annoyance and asked, "Ed, have you ever hated your mother?"

"Hated my mother? How can I hate my mother?" I looked to the others for support, but no one volunteered. A cold silence swept into the room. My gaze returned to Charley, and I snapped, "I can't hate my mother! Mothers are to be loved, obeyed, and cherished—not hated. It's a sin to hate your mother."

Again, I paused for support. There wasn't any. Tension began to take hold of me. My body was stiffening, anger was obvious in my tone of voice, and my blood was rushing to my face. I thought, could I be wrong? Have the others hated their mothers? How could they? No one seems to care. It's a sin to hate your mother. Strange feelings were welling up inside of me. A long silence prevailed. I was very uncomfortable.

Finally, I said, "Charley, my mother worked very hard, raising eight children all by herself. My father worked two jobs to support his family. He barely had enough time for sleeping. I never saw my father during the week. He only had Sundays off. My mother did the washing, cooking, sewing, cleaning, and she found time ... to make ... imitation flowers. She had ... no time ... for me?"

I didn't know what was happening to me. My saying she had no time for me and that I only saw my father on Sundays struck a chord deep inside of me. "I'd never had the chance to enjoy a father. All I ever heard was my mother telling me, 'When your father gets home, he'll take care of you for being a bad boy.' I never wanted to see my father."

Charley signaled Alice and Kay. They both made ready for whatever he wanted.

My anger was now taking over. I began to shake and had trouble with my words.

Charley asked, "Do you want the pillows, Ed?"

"NO!" I bellowed as loud as I could, "I wish I were in the pool so I could kick and beat the hell out of the water."

Again Charley signaled Agnes and Kay. They both got up, ran to the doorway and quickly came back with two mattresses. They laid them down in the center of the circle, one on top of the other.

"What's that for?" I demanded.

"Ed, we don't have access to a pool at this moment, and the mattresses are a good way to use your legs—to kick them and release your anger."

In utter exasperation I retorted, "Charley, I don't have any anger, and I don't hate my mother."

"I know, Ed," Charley calmly agreed.

I stood up. I wanted to scream. Now I was angry—really mad. I looked at the mattresses, then scanned the group. Something happened to me. I didn't know what. I didn't know how I got down onto the mattresses, but I knew my legs were kicking, kicking, and kicking. I could see them rising and falling hard onto the mattresses.

What am I doing? I thought. "I can't hate my mom."

I could hear voices saying, "Oh! Oh! Edzu, your kicking is hurting me!" The group began accommodating me. I was kicking so hard. One of the voices was saying, "I'm sorry, I'm sorry!" The one that said Edzu sounded like my mother. Those voices intensified my kicking.

Another voice which also sounded like my mother said, "OW! I couldn't give you any attention. Ow! I was too busy."

I kicked and I kicked. I tried to stop but couldn't. Something was forcing me to continue.

"OUCH!" Again, my mother said, "That hurt. I know I didn't have any time for you. Please! You're hurting me! Your kicks are hurting me bad, ooh, ooh, ow!"

I kicked and I kicked, and kicked some more. When my legs hit the mattresses, I raised my arms and hit them. Now, I didn't want to stop. I kicked harder and harder. I wondered where all this energy was coming from. I finally began to tire. My legs and arms were getting heavier and difficult to lift. All my energy had eked out of me. I could hardly lift my legs. Each kick slowed until my legs wouldn't lift anymore. Exhaustion came to my rescue. I covered my face with my arms, and I screamed, "I DON'T HATE MY MOM!"

I didn't know what was happening, but as I was taking deep breaths, a blissful feeling was settling all over me. I began to relax and didn't know it. Everything seemed to get brighter and clearer as if my eye lenses were readjusting. The chair legs, the groups' legs, the ceiling, and everything became as vivid as could be. I thought of my back. "Oh my back. It's going to hurt worse than ever, for doing this." Strange, I couldn't feel anything different in my back. It felt the same as it had when I was talking. When I talked I didn't feel the pain.

"Are you okay, Ed?" Charley asked with the greatest of empathy. He was on the edge of his chair.

I took a couple of deep breaths, afraid to move. "I think I feel better," I answered.

I lay still a while longer, relief filling my body and mind. Suddenly, I had no anxieties and began to feel relaxed. "Charley, what happened? I have never felt such comfort before. Better than the pillows."

"That's good to hear, Ed." Charley smiled.

Charley and Archie helped me get up and assisted me to my chair. My body felt like there were no bones in it, and it sank into the chair.

"Charley," I said, "I won't hate my mother," I meant it. "I love her."

"Ed, I like that. I know what you're saying. You do love your mother, but you can hate what she did. In other words, you can love someone, but you can hate what they sometimes do."

"Who said Edzu?" I asked.

Agnes answered, "I did. I'm Polish too. That's Ed in Polish, right?"

27

BIOFEEDBACK

On my way to the evening meal, I had to pass the bulletin board. My eyes quickly glanced at it and settled on a new notice. I stopped and read, "Tonight, we are to have a special exercise called "The Biofeedback Relaxing Technique." It will be held in the conference room. It would be best for women to wear shorts or long pants. All are welcomed to participate."

After the evening meal, before the biofeedback exercise, I joined Alex, Mal, and Jim in Ernie's room. We were going over the day's events when Grace stopped at the doorway and interrupted with, "Mal, your girlfriend is waiting in your room."

Mal's eyes widened, and she flew out of the room, nearly knocking Grace to the floor. It was a good thing Grace got out of her way in time. I had never seen anyone leave as fast as Mal did. I asked the others, "Who is this girlfriend?"

"That's Mal's gay friend," Jim said. "They'll lock themselves in her room, and you won't see them until nine o'clock, when her friend has to leave the hospital."

With shock and disappointment, I asked, "Are you telling me that Mal is a lesbian?"

"Yes, I am, " Jim answered. "Ask her. She'll tell you."

I left the room disheartened. I knew there was something odd about Mal's clothing. She wore clothing that men usually wear. Her haircut was more like a man's. But here in the rehab, what difference would all that make? I liked Mal. Why should I allow bias to develop into hatred between us? My mind fought the issue, but my upbringing fought back. I liked Mal, and I was going to continue liking her. I let my brain know it. I wasn't going to care about her private life. She had been a great help to me—more than any other patient.

I got ready and left for the biofeedback exercise. Along the way, I became curious about the extreme pain that always overcame me when Mal had her turn at psychomotor. Had I sensed that she was gay and had that feeling unconsciously exacerbated my pain? I was almost certain that was the case.

As I entered the room, I saw Harry. He was the only patient there and was talking to a woman. I said, "Hi, I'm Ed!" I knew the woman had to be the biofeedback therapist.

As she walked towards me, her body moved with a relaxed gait that I had never seen on anyone in the Pain Unit. She didn't show a single tight spot on her body.

"Good evening!" she said throwing her arms around me. "My name is Dorothy."

This time I enjoyed the hug. Hugging was becoming the norm for me. It was a good way to show one's openness. "Welcome to the Pain Unit," I said.

Within seconds, the room resonated with welcomes from all of the other patients. Once the group settled, Dorothy introduced herself. The patients again welcomed her. I looked around for Mal, but she wasn't there.

Dorothy spoke. "As you all know, I am a Biofeedback Therapist. Biofeedback is a mechanism used today to lower blood pressure, prevent cancer, and avoid other ailments. What we will do tonight is an exercise to relax the entire body. This is the same exercise used to start treatment with biofeedback."

Dorothy's voice was clear, easy to hear, and pitched at a tone that I could have listened to all night. She smiled as she spoke. Her posture was perfect. She was tall with light brown hair. Her hairdo was not fussy, but plain, with bangs in front and hanging straight way down her back. I listened very carefully. I didn't want to miss a thing.

Dorothy continued, "We are going to use a biofeedback exercise to completely and totally relax your entire body. You will achieve the ultimate in relaxation. Your entire body will feel better than you can ever imagine. The key to the success of this exercise is the speed at which you do it. The slower you do it, the more effective it becomes.

"What are the advantages of this biofeedback exercise?" Dorothy asked. Then she answered her own question. "I can't emphasize enough the importance of concentrating on all the details that will be mentioned and not missing a single one. You may add your own as you experience the exercise. The more details you focus on, the more aware your mind will become. It will send those details as signals to the brain, and there they will be stored. The brain will record every detail of what happens when you have gone through the entire procedure. The sharper your awareness, the keener your mind becomes. That sharp awareness and keen mind will know where the tensions have settled in your body. The mind will send signals to the brain about where the tensions are located. The brain will act on those signals and send what's necessary to relieve them." Dorothy took a deep breath and paused.

I saw that Dorothy was eyeing the entire group and wondered what conclusions she was forming.

"I want to say one more thing, and then we'll get on with the exercise. What I have just said is the most important part of this meeting. If you want to know what tensions really are, and where they settle, you must do this exercise with the same vigor a piano player would use to become a master player."

Dorothy took another deep breath and said, "First I must caution you. We will be lying on the floor. Under no circumstances should any of you rise up from the floor before you have prepared yourself to do so. First, open your eyes, scan your area, know where you are, stretch your entire body, and yawn if you can. This is very important. I have seen many people who have not heeded what I have just said. They got up, got dizzy, and some even passed out. Let's not get up without the stretching, scanning, knowing and yawning. Is that understood?"

"Okay! Yes!" and nodding, our answer could be heard and seen. We were all in agreement.

"Good!" Dorothy replied. "Now I want all of you to lie down on the floor. I see some ladies have not worn long pants or shorts. The exercise requires you to raise your legs. I hope that will not be a problem."

Dorothy waited as we found spaces on the floor. The floor became crowded, and I found it very hard on my back. Finally, we settled into our own spaces.

"I want all of you to loosen anything that is tight on your body. It's very important that tightness does not distract you from totally relaxing."

I unbuckled my belt and took off my shoes, while I kept listening.

"Close your eyes," Dorothy said. "Hitch a ride on that signal your mind just gave to the brain. Notice how fast your brain got the message and ordered the muscles in your eyelids to close. Feel the movement in the muscles that closed your eyelids and created the darkness. See and feel the darkness." She paused. "Now take a deep breath. Be a part of that breath and follow its course. Feel the coolness as it passes over your lips. See and feel its coolness as it goes over your lips, down into your lungs, and expands your stomach. Imagine how the oxygen in that air leaves the lungs as molecules, and enters and feeds the bloodstream— its most important nutrient. Notice the way the rest of your body is affected.

"Now exhale. Concentrate on the air coming out. Feel your stomach as it contracts, how the body returns to its normal position. Feel the air coming up from your lungs, then out through your mouth, over your lips, and now; it's warm. It's no longer the same air. All the freshness in it is gone and it's stale. Your mind and brain are now preparing for the next step."

I tried to do as she asked, but found it difficult to imagine all those details. I knew I was going to learn how, though.

Dorothy repeated the breathing two more times. Then she said, "Try to keep your eyes closed at all times. When they are opened, it is very difficult to create images of what you are doing. Keep your eyes closed throughout the exercise."

I thought my last breath had more imagery in it. What an exercise! It was fun to do.

"In your mind, picture your right leg from the hip down and concentrate on that whole area. Note that the brain has set in motion all the muscles, tendons, and a supply of blood to start your leg rising. Everything that is a part of that leg is preparing for the rise. It doesn't go up automatically. Now, very slowly, as slow as possible … even slower than that … raise your right leg. Notice, as you begin to move it, how your leg tightens—how the toes move and point to the ceiling—how it is touching less and less of the floor. Be aware of what is happening to your entire body as you begin to raise your leg. As the leg is moving, notice what happens to the support under it. That support is getting weaker and weaker until there is no more. Your leg, at the heel, is no longer being supported. Neither is the calf. Keep raising your leg slowly, and even more slowly. As it becomes free from support, feel the strain throughout your body. Notice how your left leg is straining now that your right leg is being raised. Every part of your body has a part in raising your leg. Be aware of that. Notice how heavy it is becoming. Keep raising it slowly. It's becoming heavier and heavier. Slowly, slowly keep raising it. It's getting heavier and heavier. You want to stop, and let it fall to the floor. It's getting too heavy."

My leg was not only getting extremely heavy, but it was creating a lot of pain in my back. I kept wishing she would stop and allow us to lower our leg. Mine was too heavy.

"Now stop. Start lowering your right leg. Lower it slower than you raised it. Feel the difference when lowering it. Feel the relief that came when you stopped raising your leg and began to lower it. Slowly lower it. That relief didn't last very long. You want to quickly drop it to the floor. But you must persist and keep lowering it as slowly as possible. You can't wait much longer until your leg reaches the floor. You're almost there. It won't be long now. There's the floor. The calf begins to touch it, and now the heel follows immediately. Keep it slow. Feel now, how the floor is coming to your rescue to support your leg and take all the pressure away. Notice that the strain put on your left leg has now disappeared. Notice what happened to the rest of your body. Your body slowly returned to its original position. Your leg now is completely relaxed. It feels as if it isn't there. It feels so good. It feels better than ever. Now your right leg is completely and totally relaxed. Yes, your right leg is totally relaxed."

My right leg certainly was as relaxed as it could ever be. There was no question about it. I thought ahead—if my leg felt that way, and we finished doing the rest of my body, the exercise will relax my entire body. What a wonderful feeling to anticipate!

After taking a deep breath, Dorothy continued with the same procedure on the left leg. At the end of it she repeated, "Your right leg is perfectly relaxed. Your left leg is perfectly relaxed." Then she continued with raising the right arm. She mentioned every detail that was happening to that arm. She didn't miss anything. At the end of the exercise she again repeated, "Your right leg is completely relaxed. Your left leg is completely relaxed, and your right arm is completely relaxed." She did the head and the torso all in the same fashion. At the end of each body part, she repeated the names of those parts that were completely relaxed.

"Now your entire body is completely and totally relaxed. It's relaxed like never before. It feels like a sack of feathers, as light as can be. Don't open your eyes yet. Feel your body floating all over the room. It feels so light. Now, open your eyes. Feel your eyelids retract to reveal where you are. Scan the area and know where you are. Stretch. Stretch as much as you can. Yawn. Yawn deeply and know you are well, alive, and feeling better than ever. The end."

There was a lot of yawning and body action from all. I couldn't believe the wonderful feeling that had come over me. At times during the exercise, my back hurt. Now, however, I was sitting up, and I didn't feel any pain anywhere. My body had never felt like this. It was loose— so loose, I felt I would have to glue it back together. It seemed to want to flop all over.

Dorothy asked, "How do you feel?"

She got a mixed reaction.

"Good."

"It didn't do anything for me."

"I slept through it."

"I couldn't do the imaging."

Different patients had different opinions.

I said, "I have never been so relaxed. Once I got the hang of imaging, it was fun. It was really something to get inside of my body. Boy, was there a lot of stuff in there."

Dorothy thanked us all and reminded us to practice it every day, to master it.

I walked over to her as if I were on a cloud, hugged her, and said, "You've delivered a gift to me that I will treasure."

She hugged me harder.

28

THE MOON AND THE SUN

On this particular day, my schedule called for a psychodrama session. In the meeting room, my group members, along with another group, had already taken their seats. We were ready.

Ms. Rede, our happy psychodrama teacher, welcomed us as usual. She began our session with, "Today we are going to do another psychodrama. As you know from our last session, psychodrama is acting out specific points in a negative manner, and then changing them into a positive one. These points will allow the rest of us to see how you come across, or how your behavior appears to others."

I looked around the room and could see that most of the patients were stirring in their seats. I didn't think anyone had paid attention to what she'd said. Most of the patients were loath to act out anything she wanted.

"I will ask for two volunteers to act out a scene in a negative sense. Again, the rest will observe and see what can be learned. After that scene, I will have them do the same drama again, but in a positive sense. They will try to show how the scene can be more effective when positive."

After going through the last session, I wanted no part of this psychodrama. I had been able to relive an experience from the past that had become very real to me, in this room. It was scary. The words had poured out of me in the same manner as they had when the event had originally happened. I had to stop. I relived Archie's kitchen scene with the same words and same feelings. It was too strange.

No one was rushing to volunteer.

Ms. Rede explained, "What I want you to do is to think of this point: In some countries, the sun is male and the moon is female. In other countries, the sun is female and the moon is male. Think about it. In the meantime, do I have any volunteers to take a part? I need one who believes the sun is male and the moon is female. The other is to believe the sun is female and the moon is male. Any volunteers?"

Only shifting of feet and bodies could be heard.

"Come on! There must be someone here who would like to participate," Ms. Rede pleaded, her ever present smile on her face. She waited.

"Mal, how about you?" she coaxed.

"Oh, all right," Mal answered. Mal was generally very cooperative. "I'll take the female moon and the male sun part."

"One more, please."

"I will," said Jim, hesitatingly, his face showing no pleasure whatsoever. "I guess I'll have to believe that the sun is female and the moon male. Now what?"

"Good!" said Ms. Rede.

She began by putting the scene into perspective. She instructed both participants to imagine standing on a bridge, gazing out into the river. The moon would be creating a beautiful sight, reflecting its light onto the surface of the water. "Remember, you have opposite views about which is male and female."

Ms. Rede asked Mal and Jim to stand by the window. She pointed to it and said, "Pretend that you're on a bridge, and the window is a river reflecting the moon's rays from the sky. You can start whenever you're ready."

A minute had passed. Mal looked over at Jim and said, "Isn't that reflection of the moon beautiful? She's just gorgeous up there in the sky." Then she gazed back at the river.

Jim turned his head immediately towards Mal, looked hard at her, and asked, "Why did you say 'She's beautiful up there in the sky?' The moon is male not female."

"Oh no," Mal said. "The moon is female.

"NO! The moon is male. You have it all wrong!"

"Wait a minute, I don't have it wrong! You're the one who's wrong! The moon has always been female. It's the sun that's male. NOT THE MOON!"

"WHAT? LOOK!" Jim said impatiently. "I don't know who told you that the moon is female. It's male. You've never heard anyone say 'the girl on the moon.' It's always the MAN ON THE MOON. The face of the moon is of a man, not a woman."

I could feel the tension and the anger building up between the two. "They're supposed to be acting," I thought.

Mal, turning toward Jim with her hands on her hips, said, "You're a damn fool! Go home and learn something about the moon!" She turned and walked away.

Jim, now almost uncontrollable, screamed, "YOU'RE THE ONE WHO DOESN'T KNOW ANYTHING! YOU'RE A SLUT! THE MOON IS MALE!" He turned and walked away.

It was all over. Now, what was I supposed to have learned from this? I hoped Ms. Rede wouldn't call on me.

"Well done, Mal, well done, Jim. You both did a good job." Ms. Rede looked around at the group and asked, "Any comments?"

There were. Some of the people said that Mal and Jim certainly took something of beauty and turned it into a meaningless fight. Neither one had gotten any satisfaction, only anger. What else was there to do when you were brought up to believe one thing, and someone else was brought up to believe just the opposite? How could you reconcile such differences?

"Yes," Ms. Rede said, agreeing with those who made the comments. "You've seen the negative view. Now, let's try the other view, a positive one." She paused a moment and asked Mal and Jim, "How do you two feel after that episode?"

They both agreed that they could feel the anger being built up inside of them. The tone of the words spoken, in addition to the kinds of words used had caused their anger. Ms. Rede asked if they wanted to continue, and they agreed to do so. After they were allowed some time to get ready, they said they could begin.

Ms. Rede instructed them to go to the same window and start the scene again. She told Jim to start with a negative role before going into a positive one. Mal was to continue in a positive role. They took their positions.

Jim started, "Isn't he gorgeous up there? What a beautiful moon! Look at the reflection he makes on the surface of the water." He looked at Mal. "Don't you think so?

Mal turn toward him and said, "It's beautiful. I agree." She paused, twisted her head slightly, and said, "You know, that's strange. You called the moon, 'he'. I was brought up to think of it as a 'she.'"

Jim interrupted, "Oh no, it's always been a 'he'."

"That's what's strange," Mal said. "We are two people watching a moon, and we both learned different genders for it. I think that's just wonderful."

Jim said, "But now that you know the moon is male, you will have to think of it that way."

"Why? Why must I think of it your way? When I was growing up, I was told that the moon was female."

"What?" Jim asked in surprise. "You were brought up to think that the moon was female? Really!"

"Oh, yes."

Jim, now puzzled, said, "I have never heard of anyone believing that. You were actually brought up to think the moon was female?"

"Yes, I was. Now what do we do?"

"You're right. This is strange. We have opposite views about a common moon. I had never heard of anyone thinking of it as anything but male. I guess I will have to be more aware of other peoples opinions." He paused. "Why can't it be female, too?"

There was a pause as they looked at each other. Mal had turned and was about to leave. Before she could take the first step, Jim smiled and asked, "Would you have a cup of coffee with me?"

Mal turned back and looked at him, "I would love to." She smiled and added, "Will it be a male or female cup?" Then she laughed.

Once again, it was all over, and Mal and Jim took their seats. Ms. Rede praised their work and asked for comments.

Needless to say, the group did agree that the second scene was more productive.

I had no problem deciding which one I liked best, but I wasn't sure that it could always happen that way. Then I thought, "Why is she doing this? What are we to learn from it? What does this 'coming across' really mean?"

29

LET PAIN IN

Jim left our room saying, "I'm taking off. I don't feel like having an ice massage this morning."

I lay there on my bed, waiting for Grace to come in, and allowed my thoughts to focus on her ice massages. Ice massages always started my day on a positive note. I heard a knock on the partially opened door.

"Good morning!" Grace said cheerfully as she entered my room.

She said it with a warmth that none of the other patients ever mentioned. I was the only one who thought her "good mornings" had a great deal of compassion in them. It only took a moment to remove my pajama shirt, turn over on my stomach, and lower my pants to expose part of my buttocks. Then I answered her with, "It's a wonderful morning, and you're going to make it better than ever with your ice massage."

She went through the usual preparations: rolling up towels and tucking them along the sides of my back to catch the ice melt. Ice, the size of a bar of soap, was rubbed in circular motions over the incision on my back and the painful areas beyond. Grace knew exactly where to rub the ice.

As the ice was being applied, my body stiffened to enjoy and accept the frigid rubbings. The more she rubbed, the more my body stiffened in response to the cold. As usual, I began to hold my breath, enjoying every bit of it. The ice penetrated the warmth of the night and awakened my dreams to reality. Every bit of it was a joy. The pain was being frozen away. I wished it would stay permanently frozen so that I could be pain free.

Grace spoke, "Ed!" Her voice seeped into my thoughts. "Why do you keep tightening your body and holding your breath?" She continued rubbing with the ice.

"To keep the pain out, of course," I said. "I don't want the pain to come in. That's what the ice massages do for me. They help me keep the pain out for a short while."

"Ed, is it numb yet?"

"I don't know. It feels so good."

She pinched the iced area and received no response. She wiped the area with a towel and began the rhythmic slapping with the palms of her hand. She finished the slapping and removed the other towels. She asked, "Would you like to have a longer pain-free state?"

"Are you kidding?" I snapped.

"No! I'm not kidding. I know how you can get better and longer pain relief."

I turned my head toward her and blurted, "Hey, come on! Tell me how."

Grace asked, with deep sincerity, "Will you do something for me?"

"I'll do anything for you! You give the best ice massages. Sometimes the pain stays away for at least half an hour. Boy! That's great. What is it that you want me to do?"

Grace seemed to be thinking deeply. She slowly suggested, "Ed, don't try so hard to keep the pain out. Let it come in."

"Let it come in?" I laughed nervously. "Come on! You must be crazy! I don't want the pain to come in. I don't want any pain. And you're asking me to let it come in. No way!"

"Ed, can you trust me?" Grace pleaded. "Please, trust me, Ed."

She said it with such warmth and sureness that I felt like giving it a try. It gnawed on my thoughts about pain. Why would she ask me to do that? How do I sort this out?

She asked me again, "Ed, please trust me." She was begging me. "I'm not trying to hurt you. It will help you. Please, try to let the pain come in."

Finally I mumbled, "I don't know how." As I said it, confusion ran through my mind.

"I will teach you how."

I gave in to her wishes. "Ok," I said. "What do you want me to do?"

Grace began, "You're a smoker, so what I am about to ask may be difficult for you to do. Take some deep breaths."

"Heck, I can do that," I said, and began sucking the air in.

"No, no, not like that! I always see smokers take deep breaths like that. Don't take the deep breaths through your nose! Open your mouth. Take in the air in large volumes. Don't suck it in as if you were sucking through a straw. Feel the air rushing over your lips and gushing down your windpipe. Then feel how your stomach seems to be expanding with that large volume of air. It will be your lungs expanding with your stomach. Feel it, concentrate on it. OK. Let's try it again."

After several attempts, she finally and gleefully said, "There, you did it. That's it. You did it."

I tried a few more times, but I wasn't sure at all what it was that I was doing right. I just kept trying.

Now she was deliberate and very careful in what she was demanding from me.

"Good, Ed! You have a sort of rhythm going on with your breathing. Now, I want you to do this: When you take in the next breath, make it a big one, hold it for a second, then begin to release it slowly, and while you're releasing it, feel your body relaxing. At the same time, allow your pain to come in."

I attempted to do as she asked, taking in another deep breath and holding it.

"That's it! You're doing it! Now, as you exhale allow that pain to come in. Picture it coming into your body. Welcome it. Make it your friend, not your enemy. Feel how friendly it really is. It doesn't really want you to suffer like you have been. Listen to it. Listen to what it is trying to say to you. It's saying it's not your fault or mine. We're in this together, and together, we will accomplish everything you thought was impossible."

I repeated it two more times and couldn't believe what was happening. I was dumbstruck. Then I heard, "Ed, do you hear me?"

Grace repeated it louder, "Ed! Do you hear me?"

"Yes! Yes! I hear you. I'm getting an odd feeling. I feel very comfortable. I don't feel any pain in my back. I'm afraid to move or say anything."

"Okay, Ed, stay in that feeling for as long as you can. When Alice comes in to do you tonight, tell her what you have accomplished. She will continue this with you and your friend"

"Grace, I just can't believe what is happening to me."

"Ed, I have to go now. Again, stay with that feeling as long as you can."

Grace gathered her things and left with a smile on her face.

I didn't think to thank her. I was staying in that feeling. It was heaven. What was more striking was that my thoughts were focusing on my pain being my friend. PAIN MY FRIEND?

As I was facing the realities of the morning, Jim walked in, not saying a word.

"Do you want to know what happened to me during the ice massage?" I asked.

"Not really. I know you will tell me anyway."

"From now on, my pain will be my friend."

"Are you crazy, Ed? Make your pain a friend. I have never heard anything so ridiculous."

"My pain has never felt like that," I said. He seemed to be deflecting my comments.

Jim said, "All I can say is I hate ice massages. They have never done me any good. I think you're being brainwashed."

I decided not to share any more of the experience with him.

I followed my group into our day's routine. The day seemed to last forever. Finally, the night arrived. Alice would be coming by, any moment now, to administer my nightly massage. Then I could share with her my experience with Grace, letting the pain be my friend. I was looking forward to this massage. I wondered if I could accomplish the same feelings with Alice.

During the day I had been preoccupied with my new 'friend' and felt great anxiety as the day ended. I knew the day had been different from all the others. I couldn't get it out of my mind and I was afraid to share it with the other patients. I felt that the coolness I had received from my roommate would be the same reaction I would get from the others. I kept it to myself. My preoccupation was well noticed.

Alice knocked on the door and entered my room. We greeted each other. I had already rolled onto my stomach. While preparing to give my ice massage, she asked, "Is something bothering you. I was told that you seemed to be deep in thought today? Would you like to talk about it?"

Enthusiastically, I answered, swiveling my head around to look at her, "I would love to share it with you. I was afraid to share it with the group because I felt they would laugh at me. I know that you won't."

I shared what had happened to me with the morning ice massage. I could feel her warmth surrounding me as I related the morning's experience, and I finished with, "Will you help me to regain that same feeling?

"Ed, we are going to get into that feeling—right now."

She helped me on my way. Soon I was back to the same pain-free and comfortable feeling that had not found it's way into my body for so many hurting years. I wanted to chain this person to me. I wanted to solder her body to mine. I wanted her to be forever glued to me. But it had to end. She left and again I forgot the thanks. But this time, I interrupted my pain-free trance and ran after her. Yes, I ran after her. I thanked her and apologized for my forgetfulness. She severely scolded me and said sternly, "Next time, if you forget, don't come running. Stay in your bed until the whole feeling is gone." Momentarily her stern visage relaxed and she smiled at me.

I had no trouble sleeping that night. It had been a great day and I was looking forward to the morning! I had a new friend. Pain—my friend!

30

ED'S PLAN

Mary and I had an appointment with Lena, my counselor, and Tom, an aide, at four o'clock on this Wednesday afternoon. We were to discuss my progress and prepare Mary for the changes taking place within me. There was definitely a change taking place within me, and she had to know about it. She was also bringing my weekly supply of cigarettes.

At five minutes to four, I began to wonder why Mary hadn't arrived yet. If it were me, I would have been five or ten minutes early. I checked my watch again. Four o'clock and Mary still wasn't here. I began getting anxious. I knew she was going to be late again.

Sure enough, at four fifteen, she walked into my room. "Sorry I'm late," she said breathlessly. She placed her pocketbook and a bag at the foot of my bed. Mary took off her coat saying, "A parent wanted to see me after school. She needed to talk about her daughter. I feel so sorry for ..."

I cut her off and said sarcastically, "What else is new? You're always late. Did you bring my cigarettes?"

"I knew you wouldn't understand," Mary said, her voice sharp as she spoke to me. "I do my best all the time, and this is what I always get from you. Sarcasm and 'did you bring my cigarettes'?"

She picked up the bag from the foot of the bed and shoved it at me emphatically. "Yes! I brought two cartons."

"Good! But you didn't have to throw them at me." I took the bag and was about to empty it when Mary said petulantly, her anger gone, "Aren't you going to hug me first!"

"Oh … I forgot," I said, leaving my drawer to give her a hug, but still holding onto my anger and the bag. I hugged her with the bag in my hand and immediately went back to the drawer. A quick thought flashed through my mind. The hug wasn't the same as it was with Ms. Rede. I wondered why. I decided not to empty the bag at that time. Instead, I turned to my activity sheet. I decided to show Mary my schedule of exercises. She read it through very quickly and was surprised that my back didn't stop me from working such a rigorous schedule. I didn't give her a chance to comment further and blurted, "Let's go find Lena and Tom!" I started to leave, not bothering to wait for her. Mary followed.

Lena saw us from the back room as we walked by the desk and motioned for us to go into the spare room. We walked around to the other wing, down past the hotpack room and the administration offices. Along the way, no words were spoken between us. Mary was in back, I was in front, Indian fashion. In silence, we walked into the tiny room, sat down, and waited for Lena and John. The atmosphere was tense. Our silence had enveloped us. We were inside a wall of silence.

Lena and Tom finally came in and greeted us. Lena smiled saying, "I'm sorry we're late. An important problem had to be dealt with." She scrutinized us very carefully and said, "You two don't look very happy. What's going on?"

"She was late. She's always late," I snapped, uncontrollable anger surfacing, my voice growing louder with each syllable. "I don't understand why she's always late. I hate it."

Lena eyed Tom. Her chin dropped and her mouth opened.

"I always start early enough so that I won't be late. Why can't she?"

Mary spread her hands apart in front of her, arms outstretched, eyes apologetically questioning, "What am I to do when a parent is concerned with their child and wants information? I'm a teacher. It's part of my job."

"I'm not talking only about today. You're late all the time. I always have to wait for you. How is it you never have to wait for me?"

Mary seemed to wilt before my eyes. Mary is about a half a foot shorter than I am. She looked up at me and said, "Oh, Ed, I'm so sorry. I just can't help it."

While Mary spoke, I could see Lena whispering to Tom. Then they both, slowly, backed into the wall behind them and slowly slid down to the floor. They sat cross-legged on the floor and began, it seemed, to pretend to play marbles. I watched, dumbfounded, at what they were doing.

Tom, with his reddish, full head of curly hair, like a permanent gone wrong, squeaked, "Mary, come on down and play with us."

"Hey! What's going on here?" I demanded. I was still angry and could not understand what this had to do with what I was saying.

Mary just stood there, not knowing what to do.

Lena looked up at Mary and urged with her arm, "Come on, Mary! Come down and play with us!"

Mary smiled weakly and got down to the floor and began playing with them. I was completely ignored and couldn't figure out what they were doing. I stood there watching a really crazy scene. Here were three grown-up people, for no reason it seemed, sitting on the floor, pretending to play marbles. None of them looked up at me. What was I supposed to do? They were acting like children. My mind repeated it again, 'acting like children'. The message was becoming clear. That's what I was doing—acting like a child. It never occurred to me. They were trying to give me the message that I was acting like a child. A warm flush came over me. I wanted to cry. I put my hand to my face to stop its involuntary contortion.

"I'm sorry ..." A tear flowed down my cheek. "I've got your message." My voice was thick. It was hard for me to talk. "You can stop now. I'm acting like a child, aren't I?" I wanted to run out of the room, jump into the pool, and beat the hell out of it.

Mary, Lena, and Tom got up off the floor. I walked over to Mary and hugged her, hoping she would hug me back. My voice cracked as I said, "I'm sorry for acting like a child." My arms tightened around her and we felt like one. This hug I loved. It was far better than Ms. Rede's.

Lena came over to us, wrapped her arms around our hug, and said, "You've made me very happy!"

Tom joined in, his arms around Mary and me on the opposite side of Lena, and squeezed tightly. There was a pause. Tom said, "It isn't often that we have this kind of an opportunity to really enjoy our work."

Mary and I left and headed for my room. I remarked about what had happened, "Mary, these people are able to manipulate me into situations where I will show how I come across. There's no denying it. I didn't realize I was acting like a child." I grabbed her hand and held it with love.

Once inside my room, Mary picked up her things. She was getting ready to go home—another parting. I walked up to her and held her tightly. I didn't want to let go. We left the room, and this time I walked her to the car. She was not behind me. I waved at her as she drove off.

Just before retiring for the night, when I was about to put the cigarettes into my night table drawer, I held them for a moment, studying them. I wanted to quit smoking. I really did. A plan began to form in my mind. I was becoming excited, exhilarated. I was going to attempt to quit. I studied both cartons and said aloud, with determination, so my brain could hear it, "I'm going to quit smoking and I mean it! Next Wednesday I'm going to quit." Suddenly, I couldn't wait for next Wednesday to come.

"Hey! I've heard that one before," Jim smirked, as he lay on his bed; he always had something to say. "You smoke two cartons a week?   You think you're going to quit? You're funny. Thanks, Ed. I needed a good laugh before going to sleep. Thanks again!"

He chuckled, turned over on his side, and started to go to sleep.

"Go ahead and laugh," I snapped. "I'm predicting that next Wednesday I will quit smoking. But, if it gets too hot for me, I will have the right to start up again!"

Jim turned over in bed, and with a loud guffaw blurted, "SEE! I TOLD YOU! You'll never quit!"

"That's my prediction. I'm going to quit smoking, but if it gets too difficult for me, I'll reserve the right to start up again. That's the way it's going to be." I finished my cigarette, put it out, eased myself into my bed, and fell asleep.

When I got up the next morning, I shared my prediction with Grace while she was giving me an ice massage.

"Grace," I said, "next Wednesday, I'm going to quit smoking"

"You're what?   You're going to quit smoking next Wednesday? You're really going to give them up?" Grace responded with raised eyebrows. She seemed a tiny bit pleased, but I wasn't sure.

"Yes, I am." I turned my body around just a bit so I could see her face. I wanted to see if she understood clearly what I was saying. "If it gets too unbearable for me and I can't take it, I will allow myself to go back to smoking."

She marveled at my prediction and encouraged me by saying, "You're going to make it Ed. What a wonderful idea, to quit smoking! Especially the part where if it becomes unbearable, you can resume smoking. It's an excellent idea to give yourself permission to start up again if the going becomes too tough for you." Her ice massage continued, and it felt so good. "I just feel certain you're going to do it. I know you are."

At breakfast, I repeated my prediction to the other patients of the Pain Unit. The reactions were mixed. I felt very comfortable with what I told them. I knew then that I was going to quit. Some patients thought it to be a bold prediction, but I was just too comfortable with my decision to allow anything negative to interfere with it. The other patients had nothing much to say. I got up and continued with my routine. The week went on as usual.

Every time I took a pack of cigarettes out of my night table, I knew I was getting closer and closer to quitting. I waited for the negative reactions to enter my brain but none came. It was almost a pleasure to see the carton dwindle down to the last pack. My comfort in the prediction was turning into excitement. By now, I couldn't wait to get to that last cigarette. The moment finally came. It came in the strangest way. I usually had my last cigarette just before retiring for the night—that very last smoke that's always needed before sleeping. Now, I was ready for bed. I reached for the pack on my night table. There was only one cigarette left. I took it out, lit it, crumbled the pack, and tossed it into the wastebasket. How convenient that was. It was the last cigarette from the two cartons Mary had shoved at me the previous Wednesday. I finished the cigarette and put it out in the ashtray, which I emptied and left it in the bathroom. I nestled into my most comfortable sleeping position and slept. The next morning, while in the twilight zone between sleeping and waking, I heard a knock on my door. I knew it was Grace, who was always prompt and ready to give my morning ice massage.

Covering my mouth while I yawned, I greeted her with, "Good morning, Grace."

"Good morning, Ed," she answered, a smile on her face. "Get ready for your ice massage."

Sluggishly, I turned over on my stomach and got ready for the ice to deliver its potent healing. She began the rubbing. I let the ice wake more of me and said, "Grace, today is my big day. You won't believe what happened to me last night."

"Try me," she said. "I'm all ears." She kept rubbing the ice on my back.

"I always have my last cigarette before going to sleep. Last night, there was only one cigarette left in the pack. I smoked it. Can you believe that? That was the last one. There were no more, none to throw away."

Grace asked with interest, "You didn't know you were down to your last cigarette?"

"No! I didn't know. Isn't that something?"

"It certainly is, Ed." Grace mused a moment and said, "Ed, there's no doubt in my mind you're going to stop smoking. You are going quit. I feel it inside of me." She finished my massage saying, "You are never going to forget this day. I'm proud of you. I am certain you'll have no trouble remaining cigarette free." She left the room.

Grace was right. I waited throughout the day for that single moment of craving. It never came. I felt like I had never smoked before. There was no need to cough nor was there any urge for a smoke. I waited for my first day without smoking to come to an end. The day went by. Two days went by. The third day went by. No urge to smoke ever arrived. I knew that I could start up again if I couldn't handle it, but the urge just never came. I gave up smoking as easily as that.

I began to think of the relief that I was enjoying. I mentally made a list: there was no need to have a pack of cigarettes in every coat pocket; I wouldn't have to have a carton in the compartment of my car or other cartons in my desk, or leave packs in convenient places anywhere else. I wouldn't have to ask Mary to bring any more cartons. I felt great! I couldn't believe how wonderful I felt! What I loved most of all was how I could share the pitfalls of smoking with my daughter and son without a cigarette in my hand. How can any parent expect their offspring not to smoke, when they, as role models, are smoking?

31

A PREDICTION

"Good morning, Lena!"

"Good morning, Ed," Lena answered, her sweet Swedish accent tingling in my ears. "It's Monday! It's been a few days since you quit smoking! How do you feel about that?"

"Lena, I don't know how to explain it. I've lived in the darkness of this world, inside this body for so long, and always wished to leave it. Now, I can't believe how this world has become so bright. My eyes keep blinking. Everything looks shiny. I feel better than great. It's even hard for me to find the correct words to describe how I feel, and how bright and clean everything looks to me right now."

I went behind the screen, took off my trousers, shirt, and undershirt. I wrapped a towel around my midsection, walked to the massage table, and laid my body on top of it.

"Hey, look! I can keep my arms on the table with the rest of this body. They're not falling off. I must have lost twenty-five pounds."

Lena raised her eyebrows and smiled, "That could be, Ed." With her hands on her hips, she waited for me to get settled.

The massaging began, and my body accepted it with delight. Although I did not want to intrude on that delight, I really did want to ask Lena for help in dealing with some of my concerns. "Lena, I need some answers about Marty." I turned my head so I could look at her. "She's been a puzzle to me for a long time. Why is she so abrupt with all the patients? She seems to lack expertise in handling of them. She doesn't treat us the way the staff does."

"What do you mean, Ed?"

"Well, for example, I climbed the ski hill with Ernie. That was a huge achievement on my part."

"Yes, it was!" Lena nodded with approval.

"Marty was the first person I met. I was so excited, I exuberantly shared my feat with her. She looked at me, and barked sarcastically, 'So what!' I was stunned. Shocked!"

Lena continued my rubbing, saying nothing for the moment. Then choosing her words carefully, she answered, "Ed, you must understand where Marty is coming from. She is ... that way. That is how she is. You must take the good with the bad. Try to see it as a learning progress."

"Lena, I don't understand. There's no excuse for her to answer me that way."

"By doing the climb, you created a great feeling inside of you. And, you immediately wanted to share it with the first person who came along. Your immediate gratification was now in progress. Marty was the first person that came your way. Her negative retort, an external one, created a bad feeling inside of you. It's most important for you to remember that your internal feelings are the only ones that count. Stay with them."

"Oh, Lena, you're right again. You're always right. I guess I have to learn how to get rid of my bad habits more effectively."

As she was massaging, I was beginning to feel odd. Either Lena was using a different method of rubbing or I was interpreting it differently. Something strange was happening.

"Lena, I need to tell you something about my trip home last weekend. While riding home in our car, I noticed that my pain began to worsen. This is not the first time. I blamed it on riding in our small cramped car. Then, on the way back to the Pain Unit, the pain lessened. When I got to my room, I was very comfortable. What do you suppose is going on? Is it the ride in the car or is it something else? Is it something that I'm not aware of?"

"That's very interesting, Ed," she said. Her voice paused, but the rubbing continued in earnest. "Again, you must remember that being home is an external experience. You are returning to the birth of your pain and its misery. Home is where it started. Your brain hasn't forgotten. But, what is pleasing to me, is the way you are freely sharing it with me. That's more than half the battle."

I felt I had to say something, but I was still troubled by the internal and external feelings Lena was talking about. I listened.

"The Pain Unit is a structured healing environment that teaches the skills necessary to deal with your pain. Along with that, you have no family responsibilities, nor the day-to-day conflicts that occur within a family. You are free from all responsibilities. On your weekends, you leave the Pain Unit and return to your household and all its conflicts."

Unfortunately, I was able to agree with her thoroughly. Sometimes, the weekends home were worse than nightmares. I never really knew why. Maybe some of this was making sense.

"That's an enormous task for anyone to absorb without feeling some kind of discomfort. When you come back to the Pain Unit, the discomfort eases because of the Unit's structure. You feel better. That's not to say your home or your family created the pain. Like many people, you were not prepared in advance for raising a family and dealing with so many conflicts. Your need for the attention that was lacking in your childhood created many of those conflicts."

I felt like an enormous burden was falling on me. Why was it that no one else in my family had to take any responsibility for these problems?

"You quit smoking. You lost twenty-five pounds. You're practicing the skills you've learned, and you feel much better. Ed, you're on your way to prove to that neurologist, that he was wrong. He said for you to go back to bed and stay there. You didn't. You fought his judgement every step of the way. I wish all my patients were as willing as you are."

I listened hard, and then, for some reason, her rubbing was becoming unbelievably different from any of the other massages I had received. I couldn't understand what was happening to me. My whole body felt this strangeness.

"Lena, something is happening to me."

"What is it, Ed?"

"I'm having images of your hands doing their healing by pushing all the knots of pain out of my body."

"Yes, Ed."

Lena rubbed and rubbed. Her hands were like magic. "Lena, this is weird!"

"Tell me."

"I don't feel the table supporting me. Instead, a motion … a movement … my body feels as light as a feather. It is slowly being pushed through the covering of the table, through the table, through the floor and out into an open world full of blue sky. I feel like I'm floating. What's happening to me? It's wonderful. I have no pain. I have never experienced a massage like this one. I feel great. No pain!"

"Ok, Ed. I'm all done."

I was jolted back to reality. I pulled myself up, carefully swung my feet over the side of the table, looked squarely at Lena, and said, "What an experience!"

"Ed, while I was rubbing I felt the knots in your back disappear. You don't have a single knot left. It's soft as it can be. My hands were sinking into your skin. All those tight spots you had are now gone."

Surprised, I said, "They're all gone?"

"Yes, all gone," she said, emphatically. "Everyone of them." Her happiness bubbled all over me. I stood up very carefully and felt no pain. I hugged Lena and didn't know what to say. Only my tears flooding my eyes spoke for me. I left the room on a cloud.

During the next couple of days, my pain was easier to deal with. In fact, there were many moments when there was no pain. I became ecstatic.

Another Wednesday arrived. I joined the group at the breakfast table for the doctor's rounds. We always left one empty seat for the doctor. His rounds were generally held at the breakfast table, after we got through eating.

The doctor entered the room and sat in the empty chair. As usual, he stared at all of us, and then his eyes went right to mine and said, "Ed, you look different. You seem more relaxed." He scrutinized me very carefully. "I feel some nice vibrations coming my way from you. I've been told that you've stopped smoking. And, I can see that you've lost a great amount of weight. Lena also shared your experience on the massage table. Do you have anything you'd like to tell us?"

I thought for a moment. He must know of my newfound, pain-free trances. Without thinking, I said, "Next Wednesday, I'm going to lose my pain. I'm going to be pain free. And, that is so!" I sat back in my chair. I couldn't believe what my voice was saying.

There was another long pause. I was trying to collect myself. What was I saying? I was going to be the laughing stock of this Pain Unit. How could I say this? I'm sure the doctor could see the utter disbelief showing on my face. My body wanted to run, but my mind held fast. I was anxious. I repeated, "Yes, I'm going to lose my pain this coming Wednesday. I'm predicting that right now."

The doctor smiled. "Ed, I believe you. I'm looking forward to Wednesday. I feel, deep inside of me, that you have succeeded. You worked hard. All of the staff can attest to that. You deserve success."

I looked at the faces of the other patients. I was waiting for some kind of response, any kind of response. There was none. I felt and saw the same coolness that I noticed from Jim, on the morning I let my pain become my friend. I saw nothing, but blank faces. Maybe they were preoccupied with their own pain and problems. Maybe they couldn't allow themselves to listen to what they felt was an impossibility. A prediction of losing my pain? Seven days from today? That was something they could not grasp.

I know I am going to lose my pain. AND THAT IS SO!

32

PAID FOR PAIN

I went through my morning routine and met with the other patients at the dinner table. No one mentioned anything about my prediction. After I had finished my dinner, Frank, Harry, Loretta, and I stayed seated together for a while. Not much was being said, so I decided to leave. I pushed my seat away from the table and was about to get up, when Frank gruffly said, "Ed, wait a minute!"

I sat down again and answered, "What?"

"Are you aware that if you lose your pain, you won't be able to collect your Social Security?"

"You won't be able to collect Workmen's Compensation, either," Loretta added in her high-pitched, nagging voice.

"Ed." Harry got my attention. "If you lose your pain, all your benefits will be gone. What will you do?"

Loretta continued, "Harry's right, Ed. What will you do?"

I was moving around in my seat, trying to find a comfortable spot. I found these questions were disturbing me. They were ridiculous. I had trouble sorting them out. Here I was, in a Pain Clinic, working hard to get rid of my pain. Now, I was being told that if I lost my pain, I was going to lose all my benefits. The only benefits that were important to me were being pain free and going back to work. How could they possibly think that monetary benefits were more important than the benefits of being pain free? I was bothered by all this talk. I was growing angry. I began to show my anger.

"Look, I am more interested in becoming pain free. I want to go to work. I want to be self-sufficient. I don't want my pain!"

Frank broke in with a stabbing remark, "Ed, you know what insurance companies are like. As soon as they find out that you have lost your pain, they're going to cut you off. Our doctor has to send a report to them about our progress. If you have no pain, then you don't need your compensation."

Loretta deplored my disagreement. She whined, "The insurance companies don't give a damn about us. They're out to get us. That's how they make their money. As soon as they find out about you, they'll cut you off. Immediately."

I didn't allow myself to hear anymore of what they were saying. I interrupted them rudely by saying, "I have to go to P.T. now. I'll see you!"

That whole incident bothered me. I tried to shelve it, but had difficulty doing so. I decided to bring it up at my next psychomotor session. That decision eased my mind. It allowed me to concentrate only on my future, and how wonderful it was going to be. I would be home with my family. I would be able to work. Life would begin to be easier for all of us at home. I began to think of the ice massages, and of what they were doing for me. I thought of Wednesday, my wonderful Wednesday, the beginning of my pain-free days!

After Physical Therapy, I went to my psychomotor session. I wanted to be the first one, this time. I needed to clarify the after-dinner encounter. I had to settle it once and for all. I needed a clearer mind, so I could continue on to pain-free days.

Once we had settled, and before anyone could say anything, I stared at Charley and said, rather nervously, "At the dinner table, I was told by my friends that if I lose my pain, I will lose all my benefits. They told me I would no longer receive Workmen's Compensation and Social Security money. I argued with them. I grew quite angry. I told them being pain free was far more important than the money I was receiving. What's going on here, Charley? Are we talking about money or pain?"

Charley always took a long time to come up with a response. When he did come up with one, it was always the correct one. He had this uncanny way of holding you spellbound with his compassionate eyes. I just knew whatever he was going to say or do would be most useful to me.

I was right. He asked me questions that enlightened me about how I had created a negative atmosphere with my friends. Charley felt they were only trying to caution me and to sharpen my awareness to any pitfalls, due to a pain-free state. I had not focussed in on all the good points. I did see the value in what he pointed out. I vowed I would be more objective with my thoughts. I gazed steadily at the floor in deep thought. Silence enveloped me. I looked up once again and saw his beard move. I waited for the sounds to penetrate. I knew my face fell once again. The words actually reverberated through my body.

"Do you feel that you're being paid to hold onto your pain?"

I looked around at the group, looking for some support, or for some response. I guess I expected them to scream and holler at such a demeaning and pointed question. They, too, were in pain. They were also receiving the same insurance benefits that I was. If I was sitting around, keeping my pain for the checks, then they too must be doing the same. I lost all faith in Charley. What the hell was he trying to do to me? That question exacerbated my pain to the extent that I thought, "Good-bye Wednesday." I would never again see a pain-free state. And now, all he was doing was sitting there behind his beard, with eyes that looked like they had turned icy cold. Why did he do this to me? I was gravely displeased. I was very angry, once again.

"Ed, you seem quite upset at what I asked."

"You had better believe it ... I am upset. I'M VERY UPSET," I screamed. I was rigid with anger.

My eyes began to fill up. At first, I fought back the tears. But, they had taught me here to allow the tears to flow. I did just that. I let them flow, asking how he could judge me like that. I didn't want to be paid for my pain. I wasn't that type of person. Didn't he know me well enough by now?

I stared into his eyes. The icy coldness ... it wasn't there. Confusion beset me. I knew I had seen icy cold eyes. Then it dawned on me. Again, I had allowed my negative side to overtake my thinking. He would never try to hurt me. Not Charley. The compassion was always there, just flowing out of those eyes. I'd put up the barrier and had lost my objectivity for that moment. My eyes were blinded. I had not seen his flow of compassion, trying to break down that barrier I had used to protect me. Now, I could see how I used it to protect my negative thoughts. Charley had his reasons for that question. Reasons I didn't know. For a moment, I had lost my trust in him. I still didn't really know what that question meant, but I was beginning to feel a bit better.

"What's going on now, Ed?" Charley wanted to know.

His eyes inundated me with his compassion. I said, "I'm sorry, Charley. I let my negativity get the best of me. I know you have a reason for that question. I know that soon I will understand what it really means. Right now, I am just confused and discouraged."

"I know, Ed. But you are doing just fine. In good time, we will sort this out. I am not quite sure what it means either. But you did show some genuinely good emotions. That is what is more important. You created the situation, and you worked yourself out of it. You have had a good session. What about this Wednesday's pain-free business that I am hearing about? Do you want to talk about that?"

I shared with him my experiences with the ice massage, and the regular massage. I added, "I just feel that this Wednesday I am going to lose my pain. I feel so strongly about that. I don't want to say it, but it keeps coming out. Wednesday I am going to lose my pain. There. I've said it again."

"I believe you Ed. I'm willing to bet on it." Charley looked at his watch. "We must stop now. Ed, this was a good session. How do you feel about it?"

"I've already said it. Wednesday, I am going to lose my pain. I feel great."

33

PAIN FREE

"Come in!" I said.   It was Grace, ready to apply my morning ice massage.

She spoke with her usual friendliness. "It's Wednesday, Ed. Have you checked with your 'friend' this morning?"

"No, I haven't. But I feel very comfortable right now. I'll know better when I get dressed. I feel certain there'll be no pain."

She finished my ice massage and said, "Ed, I know you're going to be pain-free today." She gathered her paraphernalia and left.

I started my usual morning ritual of washing, shaving, tooth brushing, and dressing. I kept anticipating pain. It didn't come. After each chore, I wondered why I didn't have any pain. Was it all in my mind?

I knew my roommate was aware of my prediction. Now that it was happening, I wanted to share it with him. However, I wasn't comfortable in doing so. I knew he would sneer and be skeptical. I left it as if nothing unusual were happening. He didn't ask if I was pain free.

I was ready to go to breakfast. All kinds of concerns and anxieties were going through my mind. I wanted to share my feelings with my friends. I was pain free! My big moment had arrived. I didn't feel free to tell any of the patients though; I decided not to reveal my feelings to anyone. I would keep my emotions to myself, and only answer questions if asked. Why did I feel that way?

Marion was on her way to breakfast. I met her in the hallway. Stolidly, she said, "Is it gone?"

I knew her pain had complete control over her. I answered, wide-eyed, smiling, nodding, "Yes! Up to now, no pain."

"Oh," she answered curtly, while walking away, no smile on her face.

I followed her to breakfast, trying to sort out all the thoughts coursing rapidly through my mind. How would I greet those who would be in the breakfast room? I was ecstatically happy, but anxious. I walked in, saying, in my usual good-humored manner, "Good morning, everyone!" No one answered me. The same complaints, heard so often at breakfast, were still there. No one asked if I was pain free. They didn't seem to care.

I sat down at the table, listened, ate, and waited for doctor's rounds. I could barely contain my excitement.

The doctor and Kay entered the dining room. He seated himself in his usual chair, as did Kay. His immediate attention went to me. "Well, ED! How are you today?"

I grinned so wide my mouth stretched, and it hurt. Above the hurt, I vehemently said, "I AM PAIN FREE!" I repeated, "YES! I AM PAIN FREE!"

A grin broke out on his face. He jumped up from his chair to shake my hand "That's great news! I knew you would do it. Remember the interview at the time of your application? I predicted you would be one of the patients to leave pain free. You didn't let me down. I am so proud of you, Ed."

I was sitting ten feet tall. My face was grinning from ear to ear. Marvelous feelings were going through me. Everyone in the room looked gorgeous, shiny, and new. It was a time for celebrating. However, there were only a couple of patients who wanted to celebrate with me. I was puzzled. The other patients just sat there, with no expressions at all. I felt they didn't believe me. Maybe, when I asked the doctor for a contract, they would change their minds.

I waited for silence and searched deeply into my mind to make sure I could handle all obstacles that might get in my way. I remembered others who, when they were in the same situation and made their request for a contract, ran into many physical problems. They didn't succeed. Now it was my turn. This was my moment. I had to make my request. I said loudly, "I WANT A CONTRACT!" They probably heard me on the first floor.

I said once again, "I WANT A CONTRACT!"

The doctor wasn't surprised when he heard my request. He asked, "When do you want it to start, Ed?"

"Immediately! I want to start right now! I want two weeks to detox and one week free."

"Good! I'll write up the orders as soon as we get through with these rounds."

He turned to Kay and said, "Make a note of Ed's request for detox."

"It's already been noted, Doctor," she said.

The rounds continued. My thoughts ran rampant from my pain-free state to those elephant capsules that would contain diminishing doses of my medication. The sugar, as a substitute, would increase until the capsule was filled with it. Good riddance to those huge dosages of painkillers I was taking.

I tried to be a part of the rounds, but instead, a host of questions passed through my mind. How would I feel when all my medication was gone? What about working? What about my no drinking and no smoking? Would I be able to continue that way? How would I feel? How would I handle my new image with my family and friends? Most important, would they be able to accept Ed? Should I go back to school?

"Rounds are over." It was a relief to hear.

As they were leaving, I was again complimented for my hard work by the doctor and Kay, who wished me well. I got up and prepared for my next activity.

On my way to the rap session, questions kept returning like boomerangs. I was able to interrupt them with a brief thought of something said in one of the sessions—"goals." Yes, "goals." I knew that was very important. Goals, I must set a goal. I must have something to work for, but I didn't know what. But for some reason, I knew a goal would eventually come to me. I entered the room, sat down, and waited.

More questions surfaced. Would I be able to deal with responsibilities? I had none here. The whole load at home was on Mary, my wife. How would I be able to help her? How could I set up a routine exercise program? Would I stick to it? Could I get my family to participate? The ice and body massages, would they learn to apply them and accept them for themselves? Would every day stresses on the outside bring back my pain? I needed these questions to stop. My mind was flying all over the place. With great effort, I made myself concentrate on the rap session.

I heard a question, "When you get home, Ed, it's going to be very different than it is here. You're not going to have the same support. Are you aware of that?"

I turned to the questioner: it was Marion. For the first time, I did some hard thinking before answering. This time the words didn't just spurt out. I knew what I wanted her to hear.

I answered, "Yes, I do know. Living at home will be very different. The type of support I enjoy here will not be available. I intend to continue with the Out Patient Facility. They will help me through the transition stages. They will be my support group. Also, I will be seeing Charley once a week. My pain and I are going to be friends. And, that is so!"

Agnes looked so pleased. She remarked, "That same question is always asked of everyone on detox. It's no surprise to me how many patients have fallen back into their same routine, as if they had never been to the Pain Unit. However, your answer is full of confidence. I'm betting you will remain pain free, Ed." The session ended.

I went to my room and prepared for pool therapy. I couldn't wait to get into that 96-degree water and to bathe in it. I walked to the pool alone. I entered the dressing room, put on my bathing suit, and wondered where everyone was. I found them all in the water. I scanned all the faces, but no one acknowledged my presence. No one had anything to say. Cheryl wasn't there to take charge. What was happening? Instead, a hospital member took the duty. She didn't introduce herself, and just sat there in a beach chair, watching. Worst of all, we didn't play with the ball. After the rap sessions, some patients were all worked out. Maybe the patients just wanted to be within their own thoughts. I felt I was completely alone. It was a strange feeling to be all alone here.

"All out!" The command came across as a dull thud. We got out, went to our respective dressing rooms, and later met in the dining hall.

When I got to the dining hall, my usual place was occupied. I found another at the end of the table and gazed out the window to daydream. I allowed some dreams to linger a while. I wondered how I could share this pain-free state with others? How could I accomplish it? How could I convince anyone, especially those patients who were here? I know that for the program to be successful, barriers must be torn down. The patients must listen and fully participate in the program. How could I convince them to do as I had done, ridding myself of those barriers? I'd started with an open mind, trying every skill put forth. It worked. Everything worked beautifully. I wanted to share how I became pain free with everyone. But how?

Next on my schedule was my body massage. For some reason, it was moved up to after dinner. Whenever I think of body massage now, I always go back to that first experience. What a beautiful invention! What a soothing method of allowing the body to escape from its stresses. Yet, ninety percent of the patients at the Pain Unit thought the massage was torture.

Lena was waiting for me. "Hi, Lena," I said smiling.

"Hi, Ed," she said in a very quiet voice. "I hear you're pain free."

"Yes, I am." I could tell by her tone of voice that something was bothering her. As Lena began rubbing me, I asked, "Is something wrong, Lena?"

"I'm sorry, Ed. I'm very preoccupied. I had to attend a staff meeting. That's why you were moved to this time."

Trying to look at her, I interrupted, "Is that why Cheryl wasn't at the pool?"

"Yes, she was at the meeting," Lena continued. "The Pain Unit has to move to another location. I don't know if you're aware of it. There will be no massaging or pool at the new Rehab Center. I won't be needed. I'm very saddened by this move."

Bewildered, I cried, "LENA! Did you say there would be no massages and no pool?"

"Yes, Ed, that's what I said. And, today, you will also meet with your new counselor, Tom. You know who he is. Tom sat in on one of our meetings. He has been fully briefed and knows your status."

I was shattered by this news. What would happen to me, to the other patients? How could someone like Lena be replaced? Worse yet, this meant I would be moving to another facility, too. Everyone would be moving!

"All done, Ed." I could barely hear her.

I got up slowly, went behind the curtain, got dressed, returned, and looked at Lena tearfully. "I'm sorry to lose you, Lena. I'll never be able to thank you enough for every rub you did to my body. You have made it the happiest one in this world. You've been my angel. I'll never forget you." I hugged her and sadly left.

After my massage, I went to my room. I was disconsolate. As I walked through the doorway, I saw Jim sitting on the edge of his bed, with one arm around another patient. I could hear sobbing words. I went over to see what was wrong. Jim saw me and waved me off. He said, somewhat rudely, "I can handle it."

"Are you sure? I would like to help," I said, trying to convince him of my good intentions. He didn't accept them, so I decided to continue on with my relaxation. I needed this because of what I had just learned about the move. I lay on my bed and began my relaxation technique. I directed my body and mind into semi-conscious states of well being.

Some days had passed and on my way to an activity I met Tom. I greeted him with my best smile, wanting to say something about him being my counselor. Before I could finish, he immediately shunned me and went off in another direction. No words passed between us. I shrugged it off. I attributed it to the Unit's conflicts.

A special session was called that evening. I arrived at the meeting room before anyone else. One by one, the others came in. The patients took up seats away from me. Once again I found myself seated next to the staff. It seemed as though none of my friends wanted to sit next to me. I felt I was being treated like an object by my friends. They acted as though I didn't exist. I was quite uncomfortable.

Most of the discussion was about the intended move of the Unit. We were hearing who was going with the unit and who was leaving. We were also instructed on how to fill out forms required by the insurance companies for the transfer. We were told where the new Rehab would be. It was a home for the aged; the elderly who were sick and demented.

Going to a home for the aged struck me as odd. Were we going from a 'how to live' situation to a 'how to die' situation? I couldn't see how the two could be joined together effectively. Now we had more stress added to our already overloaded stress box. We certainly had a lot to think about. Many of the patients didn't want to move and left the Unit.

Finally, moving day came. The move certainly wasn't without incident. There was much confusion in the dining area at the new rehab. The rehab's diet kitchen was geared up for the aged and their diet needs. We found this to be altogether disturbing since our diet requirements were vastly different. Their food was terrible.

Areas for rap sessions and other activities were not as readily available. Worst of all, there was no pool and no massages. I felt as if my right arm was cut off. Losing them was intolerable, although the staff was seeking to lease a pool at the "Y".

There were many problems. Sometimes the elderly patients, who were senile or suffering from dementia, were found in a Pain Unit room. This created concern. Items of clothing were missing, and nothing could be left on one's night table. As hard as the rehab staff tried to keep the elderly patients out of our rooms, the old people seemed to try harder to get into them.

I went home for our first weekend. When I returned Sunday evening to the Unit, I was saddened to find my daughter's artwork torn up and in the wastebasket. The pictures had been hanging on the wall. They were beautiful, and I treasured them. I use to study them each night before going to sleep. I was told that one of the elderly patients was found in my room tearing the pictures. This rehab was surely a good test for the Pain Unit staff and patients. I felt if we could survive this, we would definitely be on our way to recovery.

I was bothered by the lack of understanding and compassion from the staff, and the lack of friendship from the patients. I could cope with the new rehab. I could cope with my daughter's artwork being torn up. And I could somehow manage without Lena. What I couldn't understand was losing the friendship of the staff and my former friends. No one would talk to me. I was totally ignored. The whole situation was becoming insupportable. For the first time, I felt a need to leave the program. I wanted to get out! The Pain Unit wasn't the same. I was uncomfortable with it. The whole program was in conflict. I knew of the problems besetting the Unit, but those were their problems, not mine. The only one not affected was Charley. He always knew how to handle everything. He was the only one who was able to restore my confidence in the Unit.

On Friday, all of us had to attend a community meeting. The moderator brought the meeting to order and proceeded with the schedule. When all business was dealt with, he asked, "Is there anything else?"

My roommate Jim asked for the floor. He stood up, looked down at me arrogantly, pointed his finger, and blurted out with his customary sneer, "I don't know what's happened to Ed, but he seems to have lost his friendliness towards the rest of us. Let me tell you what he did, back at the last rehab. A patient was crying in my arms, in our room. Ed walked in, and saw us. Do you think he did anything to help? He did not. He did nothing to help console him—just went to his bed."

My chin dropped. I was paralyzed. I couldn't believe the words. They were coming from my roommate. I always treated Jim like a kitten. I knew what he was like and did my best to tiptoe around his moods. His words began exploding inside my chest. The explosions cut off my breathing. I had to start taking deep breaths.

Worse, yet, Tom, my new counselor, agreed with Jim, and reinforced everything Jim had said. "Yes," he said. "I've noticed a change in Ed, too. He always seems preoccupied and doesn't act the way he used to. He doesn't have the same interest in the Pain Unit anymore."

Tom, my counselor, agreeing ... I began sinking deeper, and deeper into my chair. I wanted out of there, and fast. I couldn't believe what my ears were hearing. The fact that Tom agreed with Jim was the last straw. All those intimate thoughts I revealed to Tom at our first session, and now, here he was accusing me and siding with Jim. Lena would never have done that. Was this what happened when you developed faith in a person? Boy, I didn't want it.

"WAIT A MINUTE!" I heard myself scream, angrily. I stood up. I faced Tom. "That's not what happened! That's not what happened at all. When I walked into our room, I found Jim with his arm around a patient. I heard sobbing and immediately headed toward both of them to offer my assistance." I looked at Jim, straight into his eyes, and yelled, "YOU WAVED ME OFF! You told me you would take care of it yourself. You told me you could handle it! What was I supposed to do?"

Never had I felt such wrath. I surprised myself at the control I was maintaining and my excellent choice of words. I felt a newfound confidence building up inside of me. I couldn't believe what I was doing, or how well I was doing it. Suddenly, there was a long pause. I was silent for a moment, gathering strength.

I found my voice and courage once again and stated emphatically, "Since the day I was able to predict that I would lose my pain, I found myself in many awkward situations. When I did lose my pain, the attitude of the WHOLE UNIT changed. I found these changes extremely difficult to sort and deal with. But I did. I lost my pain, and it now appears that I lost my friends. That is a high price to pay, BUT ... I WILL PAY IT."

The silence was never more profound. Time seemed an eternity. I sat down quietly, in my chair, with my hands folded in my lap.

My roommate stood up again. I wondered what the next accusation was going to be. I waited and stared into his eyes. They seemed strange. There was nothing accusatory about them. I thought I saw them fill with tears. He walked towards me. I wondered why? He took my hand. I stood up. He hugged me. I saw a tear.

Tom got up walked towards us, placed his arms around both of us, saying, "I'm sorry, Ed, I was wrong."

The doctor finally broke in and said, "A lesson of great importance has just has been demonstrated in front of our eyes; a lesson in daily living, and learning. Let us never forget what happened here. We may never have another opportunity to witness such an important and successful experience in human behavior. Ed! I thank you for that experience!"

Loud applause erupted from the community. I felt completely satisfied. I could not have felt better.

34

THE LAST CHAPTER

Finally my last full day at the Pain Unit arrived. Charley and I met. He reminded me of the Pain Unit's rigid structure. It would not be available at home. I told him how pleased I was at learning the skills to neutralise those stresses that would confront me. I looked forward to dealing with them and to showing them who was boss.

I made an appointment to meet with Charley every Tuesday evening for counselling. I hugged him and left. I had never hugged a man before coming to the Pain Unit. The sincerity of that hug flowed over both of us.

I headed for my last staff and patient meeting. My pain-free state still couldn't be grasped by many of the patients. The staff had no problem with it, and they congratulated me on the way in. The director of the Pain Unit singled me out, handed me a sheet of paper, and said, "Ed, would you please read this letter?"

I looked at it. It was the same letter I had written to the staff. I was shocked. He wanted me to read it.

"Will you please read it Ed," the director said.

I thought of the Gestalt experience I'd had. I took three deep breaths and began reading the letter:

To The Staff at the Pain Unit,

I would like to take this opportunity to thank the staff and patients for all the effort that was put forth by them to heal my emotional and physical states. I particularly want to thank the Director,

who seems to have an unlimited capacity for
understanding, and compassion which is shown to
all his patients. It must take an enormous amount
of strength to bear the frustration of trying to help
those who hear only what they want to hear.
That's some kind of person.

I want to thank Lena, whose hands had the
power to heal by relaxing those tension knots in
my back and legs. She is also responsible for a
good deal of the comfort I am now enjoying.

My thanks also goes to the staff. I can't seem to
find the right adjectives to truly describe their
powers. They are certainly a special kind of
people. The ability to listen to the problems of
patients, day in and day out can only be found in a
truly remarkable person.

In the short time I have been here, I have seen
numerous patients get rid of their wheelchairs,
crutches, and canes. We have our own miracles
right here. This is our 'Lourdes'.

This program has taught me, that if I exercise
my body, exercise my brain, and exercise my
awareness, I will enjoy much happiness.

Ed Guziejka

I couldn't believe it. I read it and enjoyed reading it. I
would never forget the accolade I received afterwards. I
began to feel sad because it was my last day at the Pain Unit.
I'd loved every bit of being there.

The usual business was discussed. Some problems were
solved and some weren't. The meeting came to a close, and
everyone was dismissed.

I headed for my room to pack my things. When I was
finished, I took care of all the business that needed to be
done before being discharged from the Pain Unit. I didn't
want to have any unfinished business hanging over me the

next day. The rest of the day and night, I listened to the never-ending complaints of the Pain Unit patients. I couldn't wait for morning, but I had no problem waiting for Alice to give me her last ice massage. When she finished, I hugged her hard and thanked her for the skills she had taught me. I wondered if we would ever meet again.

The next morning finally came and Grace gave me her last ice massage. I hugged her, too. Then I settled back and waited for Mary to arrive. She was on time, and we gave our farewells to all.

We were off to be together again in our own structured environment. This time, however, I had ammunition to fight back with at any stresses confronting me. My new skills would be a challenge for Mary. She hadn't learned the same skills I had learned. I expected difficulties to arise in our relationship. I was not going to be the same person who'd left home three months before. The ways in which Mary might react to my new skills would also present a challenge for me.

It took a few days to get readjusted to family life with all its conflicts. I did very well. My youngest daughter, who never slept at night, started sleeping. I would lie down on the bed with her while lightly passing my fingers over her arm, creating goose-bumps, just listening to what she had to say. I spoke only when she asked a question. She certainly had a lot to tell me. She talked about everything. My responses were positive for everything she had to say. I enjoyed our talks and looked forward to each night.

During that first night, when there was a long pause in her chatter, I asked my daughter if she would like to go into "level" as I had learned to do at the Pain Unit. She said she would love to try it.

I started her out with, "Close your eyes. Take a deep breath and concentrate on what it is doing to your body." I asked her to do it three times. Then I said, "Think of the top of your head and tighten it. Tighten it so much that it hurts. Now slowly release the tightness. Feel what that tightness was doing to the top of your head—how uncomfortable it was. Now relax that tightness slowly and be aware of the different feelings in your head." I did the same thing to her forehead, eyes, nose, mouth, and chin.

My daughter had difficulty in doing the exercise, but she tried. By the time I got to her chin, she was asleep. I said, "Go to your favourite spot with your best friends and have the greatest time of your life. Do what you always wanted to do. Tomorrow, when you wake up, you will feel better than ever before. You will have no aches and pains. You will just feel fine.

I got up and went to bed. My daughter slept through the night for the first time.

My youngest daughter was only five at the time. I knew I was not going to treat her like I had treated her brother and sister. I had treated her sister and brother the way I had been treated by my parents. I had thought that what had been good enough for my parents would be good enough for them too. They were teenagers now and were experimenting with their own lives, which was a challenge for me. I did a lot of loving and a lot of listening, and made suggestions when they asked for them. I decided I didn't have to like some of the things they did, but I would always love them. They were wonderful kids.

Using my new skills did create some conflicts in my relationship with Mary. Many times she became confused. This confusion created anxieties, and we both ended up frustrated. I knew how to deal with them. I would go for a walk, pretend to see the faces of my antagonists, and stomp the hell out of them. When I came home, I felt much better. My skills were working for me. Mary decided to get some counselling, and we were on our way.

Every Tuesday evening, I met with Charley to continue my own counselling. Charley was certainly very helpful. During my first visit, we met in the cellar of a school. He had a private room that was next to a boiler that kept the room nice and warm. There were five of us in his group on these Tuesday evenings. Charley dealt with the anxieties created by my being home. I released my anger by kicking the mattress. It was my favourite release.

My second visit with Charley was another productive one. I felt comfort in having a place to deal with my anger. This method of releasing my anger always renewed the energy I needed to move forward constructively. During this second visit, before we left, Charley informed us that the Pain Unit was moving into a new Rehabilitation Centre. He was preparing for a visit of the Director and staff of the Pain Unit. He had to set up more chairs and some tables. We helped him. He said that in the morning, he would come in early and bring some doughnuts and make the coffee. We left.

The next morning I got up and as usual I turned on the radio. The news was on, I listened. I could hardly believe what I was hearing: "There was a boiler explosion this morning at a school cellar. One person in the room next to the boiler died on his way to the hospital." Charley was that person. How was it possible? The boiler had just been renovated.

CHARLEY WAS DEAD.

Charley was an expert in his field. He was effective in manipulating his patients into situations that changed their original perspective into an effective one. He was too good at it. I wondered if that is why he was taken off this planet.

I went to Charley's wake. I met many of the staff. One person told me how people had just arrived at the school, but couldn't get in due to the fire trucks. They had checked to see what had happened, that's when they learned about Charley.

I knelt by his closed coffin and I promised him, "EVERY DAY IN EVERY WAY I WILL GET BETTER AND BETTER AND BETTER."

Thank you, Charley.

EPILOGUE

Before leaving the Pain Unit in 1974, I wrote a letter to the staff. Thanking them was most important to me. I was asked to read the letter at the final meeting of the group. Prior to being a patient at the Pain Unit, I would never have been able to write or read a thank you letter to a group of this size due to my lack of confidence and pain. They cheered and applauded me when I finished reading. I was left with warm and wonderful feelings and also the thought that maybe I could write a book describing my feelings, my struggles, my work, my pain, and my successes. I felt a strong and overwhelming urge to tell everyone in the world of my dreams and hopes for the future. I wanted all to know that I was pain free and why I was pain free. I wanted to help everyone who had back pain. What better way then in a book for all to read?

Much has happened since I left the Pain Unit and had those wonderful feelings. Whereas I'd left the unit pain free, the tensions, stresses and pressures of everyday life soon brought the pain back. While in the Pain Unit I had a structured environment. The difference between then and now is that I know what is causing the pain and what to do with it. My pain is still with me. It can never be forgotten. It follows me wherever I go. But ... I have learned to live with it. It visits me frequently depending on what is happening in my life. Thanks to Charley and his staff, I have learned to cope with it and to deal with it on a day-to-day basis.

My three children grew up. Susan and Eric were married. After they left home, Mary felt a much needed change was in order for her, hence for me and our youngest daughter, Amy. Since I was never able to return to work, I assumed a reverse role in the home. Mary, never the type to do anything in a small way, retired from 30 years of teaching in Massachusetts and worked her way slowly around the globe with the Department of Defense Dependent Schools System as a music teacher, director of musicals and drama, leader of the high school band, and drama coach for the next 16 years.

We were first sent to Okinawa, Japan, where I was instrumental in starting a writers' club that exists even today. After three years, we were transferred to Izmir, Turkey. I now know my ancient history backwards and forwards, having traveled the length and breadth of Turkey. Seven years later, we went to live in La Madalena, a tiny island on the northern tip of Sardinia, in the straits of Bonifacio. You will have a difficult time finding an island as beautiful as this one, especially the many beaches. The coastline was so irregular I was able to weave in and out with my back sculling. What a gorgeous feat for me! I've performed my torpedo back sculling in every city I've lived in for these past sixteen years. I left an impression on all who watched; they couldn't believe that my body was going forward, feet first. The best exercise for a back problem and for relaxing painful, tense muscles is torpedo back sculling! Like I said, much has happened. Our last tour of duty was in London, England. In England, we lived in a house at Gerrards Cross, on the outskirts of London, which was designed around St. George and his Dragon. I was born in the year of the Dragon, so was my granddaughter.

After twenty-five years of learning to write, I finally finished Pain My Friend. I finished it the day before the year of the Dragon was to start. Writing about my experiences at the Pain Unit was difficult. I relived the depression and all the pain that went with it. Charley ... I don't know where to begin to speak about him. Charley was so important to me. Every time I start to write about Charley my mind goes blank. I just don't know what to say, except that he was instrumental in totally changing my perception of what living on this planet is all about. Without Charley, without the

Pain Unit, without the skills taught to me there, I would never have traveled successfully around the world with my wife and daughter; I would not have been the author I am today; I would not have left a mark on many people in many walks of life; I would not have felt the successes and accomplishments I now feel with my wife Mary and my family and our innumerable friends all over the planet earth; I would not have enjoyed waking in the morning and smelling the day, absorbing the sun, thrusting myself forward to greet whatever comes my way. I am whole now. I am me. I am able TO BE, and my pain has become my friend!